BBC ACTIVE

Non fiction Gift Aid

SPANISH

Phrase Book
&Dictionary

Philippa Goodrich
Language consultant: Noelia Corte

Spanish Phrase Book and Dictionary

Based on the *BBC Spanish Phrase Book* by Carol Stanley and Philippa Goodrich,
copyright © Carol Stanley and Philippa Goodrich 1990

Published by Educational Publishers LLP trading as BBC Active
Edinburgh Gate, Harlow, Essex CM20 2JE

copyright © Philippa Goodrich and BBC Worldwide Ltd 2005
Illustrations copyright © Joanna Kerr @ New Division 2005
BBC logo © BBC 1996. BBC and BBC ACTIVE are trademarks of the British
Broadcasting Corporation

Published 2005
Reprinted 2005 (twice), 2006, 2007, 2008

The right of Philippa Goodrich to be identified as author of this Work has been
asserted by her in accordance with the Copyright, Designs and Patents Act, 1988.

ISBN 978-0-563-51921-8

Managing Editor: Joanna Kirby
Project Editor: Josie Frame
Index Editor: Paula Peebles
Designer: Elizabeth Burns
Concept design: Pentacor Book Design
Cover design: Two Associates
Cover photo copyright © CORBIS
Senior Production Controller: Man Fai Lau

Printed and bound in China. CTPSC/06

The Publisher's policy is to use paper manufactured from sustainable forests.

how to use this book

This book is divided into colour-coded sections to help you find the language you need as quickly as possible. You can also refer to the **contents** on pages 4–5, the contents lists at the start of each section or the **index** on page 221.

Along with travel and language tips, each section contains:

 YOU MAY WANT TO SAY...
language you'll need for every situation

 YOU MAY SEE...
words and phrases you'll see on signs or in print

 YOU MAY HEAR... questions, instructions or information people may ask or give you

On page 12 you'll find **essentials**, a list of basic, all-purpose phrases to help you start communicating straight away.

Many of the phrases can be adapted by simply using another word from the dictionary. For instance, take the question ¿Dónde está el aeropuerto? (Where is the airport?), if you want to know where the *station* is, just substitute la estación (station) for el aeropuerto to give ¿Dónde está la estación?.

The **pronunciation guide** is based on English sounds, and is explained on page 6. If you want some guidance on how the Spanish language works, see **basic grammar** on page 151. The **dictionary** is separated into two sections: English–Spanish (page 161) and Spanish–English (page 201).

We welcome any comments or suggestions about this book, but in the meantime, have a good trip – ¡buen viaje!

contents

pronunciation guide

✳ pronunciation

You don't need perfect pronunciation to be able to communicate – it's enough to get the sounds approximately right and to stress the words in the correct place.

Spanish pronunciation is very regular – you can tell how a word is pronounced from the way it's written, once you know what sound each letter (or group of letters) represents. A pronunciation guide is given with the phrases in this book – the system is based on English sounds, as described below.

Many Spanish consonants are pronounced in a similar way to English. The main differences are with c, g, h, j, ll, ñ, qu, r, v, z.

Spanish vowels are pronounced the same wherever they occur (unlike English, in which each vowel can be pronounced in several distinct ways).

✳ stress

Except in the cases listed below, Spanish words are stressed on the last but one syllable: tengo, gustan, España, excursiones. The exceptions are:

1 If a word ends in a consonant other than n or s, the stress is on the last syllable: Madrid, acampar, español.

2 If there is a written accent, the stress is where the accent is: estación, Málaga, café.

In this book, a stressed syllable is shown in the pronunciation guide by bold type: *estathyon*, *tengo*.

✳ vowels

SPANISH VOWELS	APPROX ENGLISH EQUIVALENT	SHOWN IN BOOK AS	EXAMPLE	
a	a in 'cat'	a	nada	**na**da
au	ow in 'cow'	ow	autobús	owto**boos**
ai, ay	i in 'pile'	iy	hay	iy
e	e in 'met'	e	cena	**the**na
ei, ey	ay in 'say'	ay	veinte	**bayn**te
i	ee in 'meet'	ee	amigo	a**mee**go
i (unstressed)	y in 'yet'	y	gracias	**grath**yas
o	o in 'lot'	o	como	**ko**mo
oi, oy	oy in 'boy'	oy	soy	soy
u	oo in 'moon'	oo	una	**oo**na
u (before another vowel)	w in 'wet'	w	cuenta muy	**kwen**ta mwee
u in que, qui, gue, gui	not pronounced	–	quién guerra	kyen **ge**rra

✳ consonants

SPANISH CONSONANTS	APPROX ENGLISH EQUIVALENT	SHOWN IN BOOK AS	EXAMPLE	
b	b in 'but'	b	baño	**ban**yo
c (followed by e or i)	th in 'thick'	th	cenar	the**nar**
c (otherwise)	c in 'can'	k	cama	**ka**ma

ch	ch in 'church'	*ch*	noche	*noche*
d	d in 'dog'	*d*	donde	*donde*
f	f in 'feet'	*f*	fonda	*fonda*
g (followed by e or i)	Scottish ch in 'loch'	*hh*	gente	*hhente*
g (otherwise)	g in 'got'	*g*	gamba	*gamba*
h	always silent	–	hora	*ora*
j	Scottish ch in 'loch'	*hh*	hijo	*eehho*
k	k in 'kit'	*k*	kilo	*keelo*
l	l in 'lock'	*l*	libro	*leebro*
ll	lli in 'million'	*ly*	llama	*lyama*
m	m in 'mat'	*m*	mano	*mano*
n	n in 'not'	*n*	nombre	*nombre*
ñ	ni in 'onion'	*ny*	mañana	*manyana*
p	p in 'pack'	*p*	pera	*pera*
qu	k in 'kit'	*k*	que	*ke*
r	rolled on the tip of the tongue	*r*	cara	*kara*
rr	strongly rolled	*rr*	perro	*perro*
s	s in 'set'	*s*	solo	*solo*
s (before m, b)	z in 'zoo'	*z*	mismo	*meezmo*
t	t in 'tin'	*t*	tengo	*tengo*
v	b in 'bat'	*b*	vino	*beeno*
x	x in 'six'	*x*	excursión	*exkoorsyon*

8

y	y in 'yet'	*y*	yo	*yo*
y (meaning 'and')	ee in 'meet'	*ee*	y	*ee*
z	th in 'thick'	*th*	plaza	*platha*

Note: d between vowels and at the end of the words often sounds more like 'th' in 'other', but for the sake of simplicity it's shown as *d* throughout this book. c and z: in Southern Spain, the Canary Islands and Latin America these are often pronounced 's' rather than '*th*'. ll is often pronounced more like the '*y*' in 'you'.

✳ the Spanish alphabet

In the Spanish alphabet, ch and ll are treated as separate letters, and there is an extra letter: ñ. For the purpose of all new dictionaries and so on, only the ñ is considered as a proper letter and appears after the n, while ch and ll appear, in alphabetical order, under c and l. (In older dictionaries, ch and ll appear as a separate letter after c and l.) The letters k and w are only found in words borrowed from other languages.

YOU MAY WANT TO SAY...

● **How is it spelt?** ¿Cómo se escribe? *komo se eskreebe*

b and v sound almost the same in Spanish. They have their own names: be for b and uve for v, but you can also distinguish them when spelling a word out by saying b como Barcelona or v como Valencia.

LETTER	PRONOUNCED	LETTER	PRONOUNCED
A	*a*	N	*ene*
B	*be*	Ñ	*enye*
C	*the*	O	*o*
CH	*che*	P	*pe*
D	*de*	Q	*koo*
E	*e*	R	*ere*
F	*efe*	S	*ese*
G	*hhe*	T	*te*
H (hache)	*ache*	U	*oo*
I	*ee*	V	*oobe*
J (jota)	*hhota*	W (uve doble)	*oobe doble*
K	*ka*	X (equis)	*ekees*
L	*ele*	Y (i griega)	*ee gree-ega*
LL	*elye*	Z (zeta)	*theta*
M	*eme*		

the basics

*essentials

Hello.	Hola.	*ola*
Good morning. *(Good day)*	Buenos días.	*bwenos **dee**-as*
Goodbye.	Adiós.	*adyos*
Yes.	Sí.	*see*
No.	No.	*no*
Please.	Por favor.	*por fabor*
Thank you. (very much)	(Muchas) gracias.	*(moochas) **grathyas***
You're welcome.	De nada.	*de **nada***
I don't know.	No sé.	*no se*
I don't understand.	No entiendo.	*no en**tyen**do*
I only speak a little bit of Spanish.	Hablo muy poco español.	*ablo mwee **poko** espanyol*
Pardon?	¿Cómo?	*komo*
Excuse me/Sorry.	Perdone.	*perdone*
I'm sorry.	Lo siento.	*lo **syen**to*
OK, fine.	Vale.	*bale*
That's all right.	Está bien.	*esta byen*
That's true/right.	Eso es.	*eso es*
It doesn't matter.	No importa.	*no ee**mporta***
More slowly.	Más despacio.	*mas des**path**yo*

Again, please.	Otra vez, por favor.	*otra beth por fabor*
Could you repeat that, please?	¿Puede repetirlo?	*pwede repeteerlo*
Do you speak English?	¿Habla usted inglés?	*abla oosteth eengles*
Is there anyone who speaks English?	¿Hay alguien que hable inglés?	*iy algyen ke hable eengles*
I'd like...	Quisiera...	*keesyera...*
What's this?	¿Qué es esto?	*ke es esto*
What's the matter?	¿Qué pasa?	*ke pasa*
What time... ?	¿A qué hora... ?	*a ke ora...*
Where is/are... ?	¿Dónde está/están... ?	*donde esta/ estan...*
Is there/are there... ?	¿Hay... ?	*iy...*
How much is... ?	¿Cuánto es... ?	*kwanto es...*
Is it possible to... ?	¿Se puede... ?	*se pwede...*
Do you have... ?	¿Tiene... ?	*tyene...*
Can I have... ? (Can you give me...?)	¿Me da... ?	*me da*
Can you tell me... ?	¿Me puede decir... ?	*me pwede detheer...*
Can you help me?	¿Puede ayudarme?	*pwede iyoodarme*

the basics

13

* numbers

0	cero	*thero*
1	uno	*oono*
2	dos	*dos*
3	tres	*tres*
4	cuatro	*kwatro*
5	cinco	*theenko*
6	seis	*says*
7	siete	*syete*
8	ocho	*ocho*
9	nueve	*nwebe*
10	diez	*dyeth*
11	once	*onthe*
12	doce	*dothe*
13	trece	*trethe*
14	catorce	*katorthe*
15	quince	*keenthe*
16	dieciséis	*dyetheesays*
17	diecisiete	*dyetheesyete*
18	dieciocho	*dyetheeocho*
19	diecinueve	*dyetheenwebe*
20	veinte	*baynte*
21	veintiuno	*baynteeoono*
22...	veintidós...	*baynteedos*
30	treinta	*traynta*
31	treinta y uno	*traynta ee oono*
32...	treinta y dos...	*traynta ee dos*
40	cuarenta	*kwarenta*
50	cincuenta	*theenkwenta*
60	sesenta	*sesenta*
70	setenta	*setenta*
80	ochenta	*ochenta*
90	noventa	*nobenta*
100	cien	*thyen*
101	ciento uno	*thyento oono*

102...	ciento dos...	*thyen*to dos
200	doscientos	dos*thyen*tos
250	doscientos cincuenta	dos*thyen*tos theen*kwenta*
300...	trescientos...	tres*thyen*tos
500	quinientos	kin*yen*tos
1000	mil	meel
100,000	cien mil	*thyen* meel
one million	un millón	oon mee*lyon*
one and a half million	un millón y medio	oon mee*lyon* ee *medeeo*

✳ ordinal numbers

first	primero	*preemero*
second	segundo	se*goon*do
third	tercero	ter*thero*
fourth	cuarto	**kwar**to
fifth	quinto	**keen**to
sixth	sexto	**sex**to
seventh	séptimo	**sep**teemo
eighth	octavo	ok*tabo*
ninth	noveno	no*beno*
tenth	décimo	de*theemo*

✳ fractions

quarter	cuarto	**kwar**to
half	medio	*medyo*
three-quarters	tres cuartos	tres **kwar**tos
a third	un tercio	oon **ter**thyo
two-thirds	dos tercios	dos **ter**thyos

the basics

✳ days

Monday	lunes	*loones*
Tuesday	martes	*martes*
Wednesday	miércoles	*myerkoles*
Thursday	jueves	*hhwebes*
Friday	viernes	*byernes*
Saturday	sábado	*sabado*
Sunday	domingo	*domeengo*

✳ months

January	enero	*enero*
February	febrero	*febrero*
March	marzo	*martho*
April	abril	*abreel*
May	mayo	*miyo*
June	junio	*hhoonyo*
July	julio	*hhoolyo*
August	agosto	*agosto*
September	septiembre	*septyembre*
October	octubre	*oktoobre*
November	noviembre	*nobyembre*
December	diciembre	*deethyembre*

✳ seasons

spring	la primavera	*la preemabera*
summer	el verano	*el berano*
autumn	el otoño	*el otonyo*
winter	el invierno	*el eenbyerno*

the basics

16

✳ dates

- Since...
  1999

  Desde...
  mil novecientos
  noventa y
  nueve

  desde...
  meel
  nobethyentos
  nobenta y
  nwebe

- In 2005.

  En dos mil cinco.

  en dos meel theenko

- What day is it
  today?

  ¿Qué día es hoy?

  ke deea es oy

- What date is it
  today?

  ¿A qué fecha
  estamos hoy?

  a ke fecha
  estamos oy

- It's (on) the
  fifteenth of April.

  Es el quince de
  abril.

  es el keenthe de
  abreel

✳ telling the time

- Use son to say 'it is' for numbers two and higher – son las cuatro (it's four o'clock). For one o'clock, use es: es la una (it's one o'clock). However, you can simply say las tres (three) when asked for the time.

To say 'half past...' in Spanish, say 'it's ... and a half' – son las dos y media (it's half past two).

Minutes past the hour are indicated in a similar way: son las cinco y diez means 'it's ten past five'.

the basics

17

For minutes to the hour, use menos (less): son las tres menos cinco (it's five to three).

'Quarter' is cuarto: es la una y cuarto (it's quarter past one); son las cinco menos cuarto (it's quarter to five).

YOU MAY WANT TO SAY...

What time is it?	¿Qué hora es?	ke ora es
What time does it...	¿A qué hora...	a ke ora...
open?	abre?	abre
close?	cierra?	thyerra
begin?	comienza?	komyentha
finish?	termina?	termeena
It's...	Son...	son...
ten o'clock (exactly)	las diez (en punto)	las dyeth (en poonto)
It's one o'clock.	Es la una.	es la oona
At...	A...	a...
half past nine	las nueve y media	las nwebe ee medya
quarter past nine	las nueve y cuarto	las nwebe ee kwarto
quarter to ten	las diez menos cuarto	las dyeth menos kwarto
twenty past ten	las diez y veinte	las dyeth ee baynte
twenty-five to ten	las diez menos veinticinco	las dyeth menos baynteetheenko
It's at...	Es a...	es a...
midday	mediodía	medyodeea
midnight	medianoche	medianoche

the basics

18

- In...
  - ten minutes
  - a quarter of an hour
  - half an hour

	Dentro de...	*dentro de...*
ten minutes	diez minutos	*dyeth meenootos*
a quarter of an hour	un cuarto de hora	*oon kwarto de ora*
half an hour	media hora	*medya ora*

✳ time phrases

YOU MAY WANT TO SAY...

day	el día	*el deea*
week	la semana	*la semana*
fortnight	la quincena	*la keenthena*
month	el mes	*el mes*
year	el año	*el anyo*
today	hoy	*oy*
tomorrow	mañana	*manyana*
the day after tomorrow	pasado mañana	*pasado manyana*
yesterday	ayer	*iyer*
the day before yesterday	anteayer	*anteiyer*
tonight	esta noche	*esta noche*
on Friday	el viernes	*el byernes*
on Fridays	los viernes	*los byernes*
every Friday	todos los viernes	*todos los byernes*
for a week	durante una semana	*doorante oona semana*
last night	anoche	*anoche*
last week	la semana pasada	*la semana pasada*
a week ago	hace una semana	*athe oona semana*
a year ago	hace un año	*athe oon anyo*

the basics

English	Spanish	Pronunciation
this...	esta...	esta...
morning	mañana	*manyana*
afternoon/	tarde	**tarde**
evening		
I'm here for two weeks.	Estaré aquí durante dos semanas.	*estare akee doorante dos semanas*
next...	la próxima...	*la **proxeema**...*
week	semana	*semana*
spring	primavera	*preema**bera***
next...	el próximo...	*el **proxeemo**...*
year	año	*anyo*
month	mes	*mes*
Tuesday	martes	***martes***
since...	desde...	***des**de...*
yesterday	ayer	*iyer*
last week	la semana pasada	*la semana pasada*
last month	el mes pasado	*el mes pasado*
last year	el año pasado	*el **anyo** pasado*
(in) the morning/ afternoon	(por) la mañana/ tarde	*(por) la **manyana**/ **tarde***
(at) night	(por) la noche	*(por) la **noche***
in six months' time	dentro de seis meses	***dentro** de says **meses***
it's...	es...	*es...*
early	temprano	*temprano*
late	tarde	***tarde***

✳ measurements

● Imperial measurements are not used in Spain – you'll need to convert distances, weights, liquid measures, etc. from imperial to metric. Speed limits and distances are always in kilometres and metres. Food is sold in grammes and kilos. Liquids are measured in litres, etc.

MEASUREMENTS

centimetres	centímetros	*thenteemetros*
metres	metros	*metros*
kilometres	kilómetros	*keelometros*
millimetres	milímetros	*meeleemetros*
a litre	un litro	*oon leetro*
25 litres	veinticinco litros	*beynteetheenko leetros*
gramme	gramo	*gramo*
100 grammes	cien gramos	*thyen gramos*
200 grammes	doscientos gramos	*dosthyentos gramos*
kilo(s)	kilo(s)	*keelo(s)*

CONVERSIONS

10cm = *4 inches*
50cm = *19.6 inches*
1 metre = *39.37 inches*
110 metres = *100 yards*
1km = *0.62 miles*

1 inch = *2.54cm*
1 foot = *30cm*
1 yard = *0.91m*
1 mile = *1.61km*

the basics

21

clothes and shoe sizes

1 litre = *1.8 pints*	**1oz** = *28g*
100g = *3.5oz*	**¼lb** = *113g*
200g = *7oz*	**½lb** = *225g*
½ kilo = *1.1lb*	**1lb** = *450g*
1 kilo = *2.2lb*	

● To convert kilometres to miles, divide by 8 and multiply by 5 e.g. 16 kilometres (16 / 8 = 2, 2 x 5 = 10) = 10 miles.

● For miles to kilometres, divide by 5 and multiply by 8 e.g. 50 miles (50 / 5 = 10, 10 x 8 = 80) = 80 kilometres.

✱ clothes and shoe sizes

WOMEN'S CLOTHES

UK	8	10	12	14	16	18	20
Continent	34	36	38	40	42	44	46

MEN'S CLOTHES

UK	36	38	40	42	44	46	48
Continent	46	48	50	52	54	56	58

MEN'S SHIRTS

UK	14	14½	15	15½	16	16½	17
Continent	36	37	38	39	41	42	43

SHOES

UK	2	3	4	5	6	7	8
Continent	35	36	37	38	39	41	42
UK	9	10	11	12			
Continent	43	44	45	46			

✳ false friends

● Many English words may sound similar to Spanish words but are 'false friends' as they have a completely different meaning. Here is a list of some of the most common ones:

FALSE FRIEND...	NOT TO BE CONFUSED WITH...
actual (current, present)	actual (real, exacto)
argumento (plot, storyline)	argument (discusión)
campo (countryside)	camping (camping)
constipado (a cold)	constipated (estreñido/a)
dirección (address)	(can also mean direction)
embarazada (pregnant)	(to be) embarrassed (tener vergüenza)
éxito (success)	exit (salida)
fábrica (factory)	fabric (tela)
librería (bookshop)	library (biblioteca)
pariente (relative)	parent(s) (padres)
sensible (sensitive)	sensible (sensato/a)
simpático (friendly, likeable)	sympathetic (compasivo/a)

✳ national holidays and festivals

● The Spanish celebrate numerous holidays and festivals, many of them religious. Celebrations tend to include a mass, a bullfight and a parade of some sort, and can go on for several days.

Many businesses close on public holidays, but the majority of bars, cafés and restaurants stay open.

the basics

Nochebuena	**Christmas Eve**	24 December
Navidad	**Christmas Day**	25 December
Nochevieja	**New Year's Eve**	31 December
Año Nuevo	**New Year's Day**	1 January
Epifanía/el Día de los Reyes Magos	**Epiphany**	6 January
San José (Día del Padre)	**St Joseph's Day (Father's day)**	19 March
Miércoles de ceniza	**Ash Wednesday**	
Domingo de Ramos	**Palm Sunday**	
Jueves Santo	**Maundy Thursday**	
Viernes Santo	**Good Friday**	
Domingo de Resurrección	**Easter Sunday**	
Semana Santa	**Holy week**	
Lunes de Pascua	**Easter Monday**	
Día del Trabajo	**Labour Day**	1 May
Día de la Madre	**Mother's Day**	First Sunday in May
Corpus Christi	**Corpus Christi**	
Santiago Apóstol	**St James' Day**	25 July
Asunción	**Assumption**	15 August
Día de la Hispanidad	**Columbus Day**	12 October
Todos los Santos	**All Saints' Day**	1 November
Día de la Constitución	**Day of the Constitution**	6 December
Inmaculada Concepción	**Immaculate Conception**	8 December

general conversation

● Buenos días means 'good morning' (or literally 'good day') and is used up to lunchtime. After that, until around 9pm or nightfall, it's buenas tardes – which means both 'good afternoon' and 'good evening'. Buenas noches can be used as a greeting late in the evening, as well as to say 'goodnight'.

● Hola means 'hello', and is often used together with one of the phrases above, e.g. hola, buenos días. Adiós (goodbye) can also be used with one of the phrases above, e.g. adiós, buenas tardes, or with a phrase like hasta luego (see you later) – adiós, hasta luego.

● To indicate formality or familiarity, Spanish uses different words to say 'you' and different endings on verbs. The formal word for 'you' is usted (oosteth) and the informal word is tú (too). There's a further explanation of this on page 156. In this book the form of address that is most adequate to each context is used.

● Spaniards often leave out pronouns before a verb. For example, they say vivo en Londres (I live in London) instead of Yo vivo en Londres. In this book pronouns are shown in brackets when you can leave them out.

✳ greetings

YOU MAY WANT TO SAY...

● **Hello.**   Hola.   *ola*

● **Good morning.**   Buenos días.   *bwenos deeas*

Good afternoon.	Buenas tardes.	*bwenas tardes*
Good evening.	Buenas noches.	*bwenas noches*
Good night.	Buenas noches.	*bwenas noches*
Goodbye.	Adiós.	*adyos*
Bye.	Chao.	*chao*
See you later.	Hasta luego.	*asta lwego*
How are you?		
(formal)	¿Cómo está (usted)?	*komo esta (oosteth)*
(informal)	¿Cómo estás?	*komo estas*
How are things?	¿Qué tal?	*ke tal*
Fine, thanks.	Bien, gracias.	*byen grathyas*
And you?		
(formal)	¿Y usted?	*ee oosteth*
(informal)	¿Y tú?	*ee too*

✳ introductions

YOU MAY WANT TO SAY...

My name is...	(Yo) me llamo...	*(yo) me lyamo...*
This is...	Este es...	*este es...*
Mr Brown	el señor Brown	*el senyor brown*
my husband	mi marido	*mee mareedo*
my son	mi hijo	*mee eehho*
my boyfriend	mi novio	*mee nobyo*
my (male) friend	mi amigo	*mee ameego*

- This is... Ésta es... *esta es...*
  Mrs Brown la señora Brown *la senyora brown*
  Miss Brown la señorita *la senyoreeta*
   Brown *brown*

  my wife mi mujer *mee moohher*
  my daughter mi hija *mee eehha*
  my girlfriend mi novia *mee nobya*
  my (female) mi amiga *mee ameega*
   friend

- Pleased to meet Mucho gusto/ *moocho goosto/*
  you.
  (if you're a man) Encantado. *enkantado*
  (if you're a Encantada. *enkantada*
   woman)

✳ talking about yourself

- I'm English. Soy inglés/inglesa. *soy eengles/*
   eenglesa

- I'm Irish. Soy irlandés/ *soy eerlandes/*
   irlandesa. *eerlandesa*

- I'm Scottish. Soy escocés/ *soy eskothes/*
   escocesa. *eskothesa*

- I'm Welsh. Soy galés/galesa. *soy gales/galesa*

- I come from... Soy de... *soy de...*
  England Inglaterra *eenglaterra*
  Ireland Irlanda *eerlanda*
  Scotland Escocia *eskothya*
  Wales Gales *gales*

- I live in...

  (Yo) vivo en...

  (yo) **beebo** *en...*

  London

  Londres

  londres

  Edinburgh

  Edimburgo

  edeemboorgo

- I'm 25 years old.

  (Yo) tengo veinticinco años.

  (yo) **tengo** *baynteetheenko anyos*

- I'm a...

  (Yo) soy...

  (yo) **soy***...*

  lawyer

  abogado/a

  abogado/a

  nurse

  enfermero/a

  enfermero/a

  student

  estudiante

  estoodyante

- I work in/for...

  Trabajo en...

  Trabahho en...

  a bank

  un banco

  oon **banko**

  a computer firm

  una empresa de informática

  oona empresa de eenformatika

- I'm unemployed.

  Estoy en paro.

  estoy en paro

- I'm self-employed.

  Soy trabajador autónomo.

  soy trabahhador owtonomo

- I'm...

  Estoy...

  estoy...

  married

  casado/a

  kasado/a

  divorced

  divorciado/a

  deeborthyado/a

  separated

  separado/a

  separado/a

  single

  soltero/a

  soltero/a

  a widower/ widow

  viudo/a

  byoodo/a

- I have...

  Tengo...

  tengo...

  three children

  tres hijos

  tres eehhos

  one brother

  un hermano

  oon ermano

  two sisters

  dos hermanas

  dos ermanas

- I don't have...

  No tengo...

  no **tengo***...*

  any children

  hijos

  eehhos

  any brothers or sisters

  hermanos

  ermanos

asking about other people

I'm on holiday here.	Estoy aquí de vacaciones.	*estoy akee de bakathyones*
I'm here on business.	Estoy aquí por negocios.	*estoy akee por negothyos*
I'm here with my...	Estoy aquí con mi...	*estoy akee kon mee...*
family	familia	*fameelya*
colleague	colega	*kolega*
My husband/son is...	Mi marido/hijo es...	*mee mareedo/eehho es...*
My wife/ daughter is...	Mi mujer/ hija es...	*mee moohher/ eehha es...*

✳ asking about other people

Where do you come from?	¿De dónde eres?	*de donde eres*
What's your name?	¿Cómo te llamas?	*komo te lyamas*
Are you married?	¿Estás casado/a?	*estas kasado/a*
Do you have...	¿Tienes...	*tyenes...*
any children?	hijos?	*eehhos*
a boy/ girlfriend?	novio/a?	*nobyo/a*
How old are you/they?	¿Cuántos años tienes/tienen?	*kwantos anyos tyenes/tyenen*

general conversation

Where are you going?	¿Adónde vas?	*adonde bas*
Where are you staying?	¿Dónde te quedas (tú)?	***don**de te ke**das** (too)*
Where do you live?	¿Dónde vives (tú)?	***don**de bee**bes** (too)*
What job do you do?	¿En qué trabajas (tú)?	*en ke tra**bahh**as (too)*
What are you studying?	¿Qué estudias (tú)?	*ke es**too**dyas (too)*

✳ chatting

YOU MAY WANT TO SAY...

Spain is very beautiful.	España es muy bonita.	*es**pan**ya es mwee bo**nee**ta*
I like Spain (very much).	Me gusta (mucho) España.	*me **goos**ta (**moo**cho) es**pan**ya*
It's the first time I've been to Andalusia.	Es la primera vez que vengo a Andalucía.	*es la pre**mera** beth ke **ben**go a andaloo**thee**a*
Do you live here?	¿Vives aquí?	*bee**bes** a**kee***
Are you from here?	¿Eres de aquí?	*eres de a**kee***
Have you ever been to... Madrid? London?	¿Has estado alguna vez en... Madrid? Londres?	*as es**tado** al**goo**na beth en... ma**dreeth** **lon**dres*

¿Te gusta España?	te **goos**ta es**pan**ya	Do you like Spain?
¿Has estado antes en España?	as es**tad**o **an**tes en es**pan**ya	Have you been to Spain before?
¿Hasta cuándo te quedas aquí?	**as**ta **kwan**do te **ked**as a**kee**	When are you here until?
Hablas muy bien español.	**ab**las mwee b**yen** espan**yol**.	Your Spanish is very good.

* the weather

YOU MAY WANT TO SAY...

It's a beautiful day!	¡Hace un día precioso!	**ath**e oon **dee**a pre**thyos**o
What fantastic weather!	¡Qué tiempo más bueno!	ke **tyem**po mas **bwen**o
It's (very)... hot cold windy	Hace (mucho)... calor frío viento	**ath**e (**mooch**o)... ka**lor** **free**o b**yen**to
What's the forecast?	¿Cuál es el pronóstico del tiempo?	kwal es el pro**nos**teeko del **tyem**po
It's... raining snowing	Está... lloviendo nevando	es**ta**... lyo**byen**do ne**ban**do

general conversation

32

✳ likes and dislikes

- I like...(singular)
  beer
  football

  Me gusta...
  la cerveza
  el fútbol

  me goosta...
  la therbetha
  el footbol

- I like...(plural)
  strawberries
  flowers

  Me gustan...
  las fresas
  las flores

  me goostan...
  las fresas
  las flores

- I love...
  the beach

  Me encanta...
  la playa

  me enkanta...
  la pliya

- I love...
  bananas

  Me encantan...
  los plátanos

  me enkantan...
  los platanos

- I don't like...
  the rain

  No me gusta...
  la lluvia

  no me goosta...
  la lyoobya

- I don't like...
  tomatoes

  No me gustan...
  los tomates

  no me goostan...
  los tomates

- I hate...
  swimming

  Odio...
  nadar

  odyo...
  nadar

- Do you like...
  walking?
  climbing?

  ¿Te gusta...
  caminar?
  el alpinismo?

  te goosta...
  kameenar
  el alpeeneesmo

- Do you like...
  ice creams?

  ¿Te gustan...
  los helados?

  te goostan...
  los elados

- I like it/them.

  Me gusta/gustan.

  me goosta/goostan

- I don't like it/
  them.

  No me gusta/
  gustan.

  no me goosta/
  goostan

✱ feelings and opinions

- **Are you all right?** | ¿Estás bien? | *estas byen*

- **Are you (very)...** | ¿Tienes (mucho)... | *tyenes (moocho)...*
  - **cold?** | frío? | *freeo*
  - **hot?** | calor? | *kalor*

- **I'm...** | Estoy... | *estoy...*
  - **tired** | cansado/a | *kansado/a*
  - **bored** | aburrido/a | *aburreedo/a*
  - **annoyed** | enfadado/a | *enfadado/a*

- **What do you think of...?** | ¿Qué te parece...? | *ke te parethe...*

- **I think it's...** | Me parece... | *me parethe...*
  - **great** | genial | *hhenyal*
  - **funny** | gracioso/a | *gratheeoso/a*

- **Did you like it?** | ¿Te gustó? | *te goosto*

- **I thought it was...** | Me pareció... | *me paretheeo...*
  - **beautiful** | precioso/a | *prethyoso/a*
  - **fantastic** | fantástico/a | *fantasteeko/a*
  - **dreadful** | horroroso/a | *orroroso/a*

- **Don't you like it?** | ¿No te gusta? | *no te goosta*

- **Do you like him/her?** | ¿Te cae bien (él/ella)? | *te kae byen (el/elya)*

- **I like him/her.** | (Él/Ella) me cae bien. | *(el/elya) me kae byen*

What is your favourite... ?	¿Cuál es tu ... preferido/a?	kwal es too ... prefereedo/a?
music	música	mooseeka
film	película	peleecoola
My favourite ... is...	Mi ... preferido/a es...	mee ... prefereedo/a es...

* making arrangements

YOU MAY WANT TO SAY...

What are you doing tonight?	¿Qué haces esta noche?	ke athes esta noche
Would you like...	¿Quieres...	kyeres...
a drink?	tomar algo?	tomar algo
something to eat?	comer algo?	komer algo
to go out?	salir?	saleer
Yes, please.	Sí, por favor.	see, por fabor
No, thank you.	No gracias.	no grathyas
I'd love to.	Me encantaría.	me enkantareea
What time shall we meet?	¿A qué hora nos vemos?	a ke ora nos bemos
Where shall we meet?	¿Dónde nos vemos?	donde nos bemos
See you...	Hasta...	asta...
later	luego	lwego
at seven	las siete	las syete

● I'm looking forward to it.	Tengo muchas ganas.	*tengo **moo**chas **ganas***
● Sorry, I already have plans.	Lo siento, pero ya tengo otros planes.	*lo **syen**to, pero ya tengo otros **planes***
● Please go away.	Por favor, váyase.	*por fa**bor**, bi**ya**se*
● Leave us alone!	¡Déjenos en paz!	*de**hhe**nos en path*

* useful expressions
(see **essentials**, pages **12–13**)

YOU MAY WANT TO SAY...

Congratulations!	¡Enhorabuena!	*enora**bwe**na*
Happy Birthday!	¡Feliz Cumpleaños!	*fe**leeth** koomple**an**yos*
Happy Christmas!	¡Feliz Navidad!	*fe**leeth** nabee**dad***
Happy New Year!	¡Feliz Año Nuevo!	*fe**leeth** anyo **nwe**bo*
Good luck!	¡Buena suerte!	***bwe**na **swer**te*
That's fantastic!	¡Qué bien!	*ke byen*
That's terrible!	¡Qué mal!	*ke mal*
What a pity!	¡Qué pena!	*ke **pe**na*
If only!	¡Ojalá!	*oh**ha**la*
Have a good journey!	¡Buen viaje!	*bwen **bya**hhe*
Enjoy your meal!	¡Qué aproveche!	*ke apro**be**che*
Thank you, same to you.	Gracias, igualmente.	***grath**yas, eeg**wal**mente*
Cheers!	¡Salud!	*sa**lood***

travel&transport

✱ arriving in the country

 Whether you arrive by air, road or sea, the formalities (passport control and Customs) are quite straightforward. The only document EU residents need is a valid passport. If you plan to stay more than 90 days you need a residence permit, which can be obtained from Police Stations. All other foreign nationals should contact the Spanish Consulate in their country of origin.

YOU MAY SEE...

Aduana	**Customs**
Artículos que declarar	**Goods to declare**
Ciudadanos comunitarios	**EU citizens**
Ciudadanos no comunitarios	**Non-EU citizens**
Control de pasaportes	**Passport control**
Recogida de equipaje	**Baggage reclaim**
Salida	**Exit**

YOU MAY WANT TO SAY...

- I am here...
  on holiday
  on business

  Estoy aquí...
  de vacaciones
  en viaje de
  negocios

  estoy akee...
  de bakathyones
  en byahhe de
  negothyos

- It's for my own
  personal use.

  Es para uso
  personal.

  es para ooso
  personal

- I am an EU citizen.

  Soy ciudadano
  comunitario.

  soy thyoodadano
  komooneetaryo

travel and transport

YOU MAY HEAR...

Su pasaporte, por favor.	*soo pasaporte por fabor*	Your passport, please.
Sus documentos, por favor.	*soos dokoomentos por fabor*	Your documents, please.
¿Cuál es el objeto de su visita?	*kwal es el obhheto de soo beeseeta*	What is the purpose of your visit?
¿Cuánto tiempo se queda aquí?	*kwanto tyempo se keda akee*	How long are you staying here?
Abra esta bolsa, por favor.	*abra esta bolsa, por fabor*	Please open this bag.
Tiene más equipaje?	*tyene mas ekeepahhe*	Do you have any other luggage?
Venga conmigo, por favor.	*benga konmeego por fabor*	Come along with me, please.

✱ directions

● When you need to ask the way somewhere, the easiest thing is just to name the place you're looking for and add 'please', e.g. ¿Granada, por favor? Or you can start with 'where is...?': ¿dónde está...?

● To ask the question 'where is the nearest...?', just ask 'is there a ... around here': ¿hay un/una ... por aquí?

● If you need someone to repeat some directions, simply say otra vez (again).

YOU MAY SEE...

Al/A la...	To the...
Alcázar	Fortress
Avenida	Avenue
Calle	Street
Carril para bicicletas	Cycle path
Castillo	Castle
Catedral	Cathedral
Estación	Station
Estación central	Main station
Galería de arte	Art gallery
Iglesia	Church
Mercado	Market place
Metro	Underground/tube
Museo	Museum
Palacio	Palace
Parada de autobuses	Bus stop
Parada de tranvía	Tram stop
Parada del metro	Tube stop
Paseo	Avenue
Paso de peatones/ Paso de cebra	Pedestrian/ Zebra crossing
Peatón/Peatones	Pedestrians
Plaza	Square
Prohibido aparcar	No parking
Prohibido el paso	No trespassing
Propiedad privada	Private property
Zona peatonal	Pedestrian precinct

- Excuse me, please.   Perdone (por favor).   *perdone (por fabor)*

- Where is...   ¿Dónde está...   *donde esta...*
    the tourist   la oficina de   *la ofeetheena de*
        centre?   turismo?   *tooreesmo*
    the station?   la estación   *la estathyon*
    the cash point?   el cajero?   *el kahhero*

- Where are the   ¿Dónde están los   *donde estan los*
  toilets?   servicios?   *serbeethyos*

- How do we get   ¿Cómo se llega...   *komo se lyega...*
  to...
    the airport?   al aeropuerto?   *al aeropwerto*
    the beach?   a la playa?   *a la pliya*

- I'm lost.   Estoy perdido/a.   *estoy perdeedo/a*

- We're lost.   Estamos perdidos/as.   *estamos perdeedos/as*

- Is this the right   ¿Vamos bien para... ?   *bamos byen para...*
  way to... ?

- Can you show   ¿Me lo puede   *me lo pwede*
  me on the map,   mostrar en el   *mostrar en el*
  please?   mapa?   *mapa*

- Is it far?   ¿Está lejos?   *esta lehhos*

- Is there ... near   ¿Hay ... cerca de   *iy ... therca de akee*
  here?   aquí?
    a bank   un banco   *oon banko*
    an internet café   un cibercafé   *oon theeberkafe*

- Where is   ¿Dónde está el   *donde esta el*
  the nearest   restaurante/bar   *restowrante/bar*
  restaurant/bar?   más cercano?   *mas therkano*

YOU MAY HEAR...

Estamos aquí.	*estamos akee*	We are here.
Por aquí/allá.	*por akee/alya*	This way/That way.
Todo recto.	*todo rekto*	Straight on.
Siga...	*seega...*	Go on...
hasta el final de la calle	*asta el feenal de la kalye*	to the end of the street
hasta el semáforo	*asta el semaforo*	to the traffic lights
Gire...	*hheere...*	Turn...
(a la) derecha	*(a la) derecha*	(to the) right
(a la) izquierda	*(a la) eethkyerda*	(to the) left
Tome la primera a la derecha.	*tome la preemera a la derecha*	Take the first on the right.
Está...	*esta...*	It's...
delante (de ...)	*delante (de...)*	in front (of...)
en frente (de...)	*en frente (de...)*	opposite
detrás (de...)	*detras (de...)*	behind
cerca (de...)	*therka (de...)*	close (to...)
al lado (de...)	*al lado (de...)*	next to...
Está (muy) cerca/ lejos.	*esta (mwee) therka/ lehhos*	It's (very) near/far away.
Está a cinco minutos.	*esta a theenko meenootos*	It's five minutes away.
Hay que tomar el autobús número...	*iy ke tomar el owtoboos noomero...*	You have to take bus number...

✱ information and tickets
(see **telling the time**, page 17)

(see **telling the time**, page 17)

YOU MAY WANT TO SAY...

Is there a train/bus/boat to ... today?	¿Hay un tren/autobús/barco para ... hoy?	*iy oon tren/owtoboos/barko para ... oy*
What time is the...	¿A qué hora es el...	*a ke ora es el...*
next train	próximo tren	*prokseemo tren*
last train	último tren	*oolteemo tren*
first bus	primer autobús	*preemer owtoboos*
...to Seville?	...para Sevilla?	*...para sebeelya*
Do they go often?	¿Son frecuentes?	*son frekwentes*
What time does it arrive in... ?	¿A qué hora llega a... ?	*a ke ora lyega a...*
Do I have to change?	¿Tengo que hacer trasbordo?	*tengo ke ather trasbordo*
Which platform for... ?	¿Cuál es el andén para... ?	*kwal es el anden para...*
Which bus stop for... ?	¿Cuál es la parada del autobús para... ?	*kwal es la parada del owtoboos para...*
Can I get a ticket on the bus/train/boat?	¿Puedo comprar un billete en el autobús/tren/barco?	*pwedo comprar oon beelyete en el owtoboos/tren/barko*
Where can I buy...	¿Dónde puedo comprar...	*donde pwedo komprar...*
a ticket?	un billete?	*oon beelyete*
a season ticket?	un abono?	*oon abono*

● **One/two tickets to ... please.**	Uno/dos billete(s) para ... (por favor).	*oono/dos beelyete(s) para ... (por fabor)*
● **single**	ida solamente	*eeda solamente*
● **return**	ida y vuelta	*eeda ee bwelta*
● **For...**	Para...	*para...*
two adults and	dos adultos y	*dos adooltos ee*
two children and a car	dos niños y un coche	*dos ninyos ee oon koche*
● **I want to reserve...**	Quiero reservar...	*kyero reserbar...*
a seat	un asiento	*oon asyento*
a cabin	un camarote	*oon kamarote*
● **Is there a...**	¿Hay algún...	*iy algoon...*
supplement?	suplemento?	*sooplemento*
reduction for students?	descuento para estudiantes?	*deskwento para estdoodyantes*

YOU MAY HEAR...

● Sale a las...	*sale a las...*	It leaves at...
● Llega a las ...	*lyega a las...*	It arrives at...
● Tiene que cambiar.	*tyene ke kambyar*	You have to change.
● Es el andén número cuatro.	*es el anden noomero kwatro*	It's platform number four.
● Puede comprar un billete...	*pwede komprar oon beelyete...*	You can buy a ticket...
en el autobús/ tren/barco.	en el owtoboos/ tren/barko	on the bus/ train/boat
en la estación	*en la estathyon*	at the station

travel and transport

44

¿De ida o de ida y vuelta?	*de ee*da *o de ee*da *ee bwel*ta	Single or return?
¿Fumador o no fumador?	*foomador o no foomador*	Smoking or non-smoking?

* trains
(see **information and tickets**, page 43)

 The Spanish State railway company is called RENFE *(renfe)*. There are RENFE offices in every city where you can get information and book tickets. You can also get information, book and buy tickets at train stations, travel agencies and tourist offices. RENFE has a website (www.renfe.es) with information in English.

YOU MAY SEE...

A los andenes	To the platforms
Andén	Platform
Billetes	Tickets
Coche cama	Sleeping-car
Compartimentos para el equipaje	Luggage lockers
Consigna (de equipajes)	Left luggage
Destino	Destination
Diario	Daily
Días laborables	Monday to Saturdays
Domingos y festivos	Sundays and holidays

trains

Entrada	Entrance
Horario de trenes	Train timetable
Huelga	Strike
Llegadas	Arrivals
Objetos perdidos	Lost property
Procedencia	Where from
Reservas	Reservations
Retraso	Delay
Sala de espera	Waiting room
Salida	Departure/exit
Servicios	Toilets
Taquilla	Ticket Office
Venta anticipada	Advance booking

YOU MAY WANT TO SAY...

- **Are there lifts to the platform?** ¿Hay ascensores a los andenes? *iy asthensores a los andenes*

- **Does this train go to... ?** ¿Este tren va a... ? *este tren ba a...*

- **Excuse me, I've reserved that seat.** Perdone, he reservado ese asiento. *perdone, e reserbado ese asyento*

- **Is this seat taken?** ¿Está ocupado este asiento? *esta okoopado este asyento*

- **May I...** ¿Puedo... *pwedo...*
  - **open the window?** abrir la ventana? *abreer la bentana*
  - **smoke?** fumar? *foomar*

● **Where are we?**	¿Dónde estamos?	*donde estamos*
● **How long does the train stop here?**	¿Durante cuánto tiempo está el tren parado aquí?	*doorante kwanto tyempo esta el tren parado akee*
● **Can you tell me when we get to... ?**	¿Me puede avisar cuando lleguemos a... ?	*me pwede abeesar kwando lyegemos a...*

✳ buses and coaches
(see **information and tickets**, page 43)

(see **information and tickets**, page 43)

YOU MAY SEE...

Autocar	Coach
Entrada	Entrance
Estación de autobuses	Bus station
No fumar	No smoking
No hablar con el conductor	Do not talk to the driver
Parada discrecional	Request stop
Parada (de autobús)	Bus stop
Prohibido salir/entrar	No exit/entry
Salida de emergencia	Emergency exit

YOU MAY WANT TO SAY...

● **Where does the bus to the (town) centre leave from?**	¿De dónde sale el autobús para el centro (de la ciudad)?	*de donde sale el owtoboos para el thentro de la thyoodad*

- **Does the bus to the airport leave from here?**   ¿Sale de aquí el autobús para el aeropuerto?   *sale de akee el owtoboos para el aeropwerto*

- **What number is it?**   ¿Qué número es?   *ke noomero es*

- **Does this bus go to... ?**   ¿Este autobús va a... ?   *este owtoboos ba a...*

- **Can you tell me where to get off, please?**   ¿Me puede decir dónde me tengo que bajar?   *me pwede detheer donde me tengo ke bahhar*

- **The next stop, please.**   La próxima parada, por favor.   *la prokseema parada, por fabor*

- **Can you open the doors please?**   ¿Puede abrir la puerta, por favor?   *pwede abreer la pwerta por fabor*

* underground
(see **information and tickets**, page 43)

YOU MAY SEE...

Entrada	Entrance
Información	Information
Metro	Underground
Prohibido fumar	No smoking
Salida	Exit

YOU MAY WANT TO SAY...

- **Do you have a map of the underground?**   ¿Tiene un plano del metro?   *tyene oon plano del metro*

travel and transport

48

● **Which line is it for the airport?**	¿Qué línea es para ir al aeropuerto?	*ke leenea es para eer al aeropwerto*
● **Which stop is it for the ... museum?**	¿Qué parada es para el ... museo?	*ke parada es para el ... mooseo*
● **Is this the right stop for... ?**	¿Es ésta la parada para... ?	*es esta la parada para...*
● **Does this train go to... ?**	¿Este metro va a... ?	*este metro ba a...*

✳ boats and ferries
(see **information and tickets**, page 43)

YOU MAY SEE...

Aerodeslizador	Hovercraft
Barcos	Boats
Barco a vapor	Steamer
Bote salvavidas	Lifeboat
Camarotes	Cabins
Cruceros	Cruises
Embarcadero	Pier, embarkation point
Muelle	Quay
Paseos por el río	River trips
Puerto	Port, harbour
Salvavidas	Lifebelt
Transbordador/ferry	Ferry

travel and transport

boats and ferries

YOU MAY WANT TO SAY...

- **Is there a ferry to ... today?** — ¿Hay un ferry/transbordador para ... hoy? — *iy oon ferree/transbordador para ... oy*

- **Are there any boat trips?** — ¿Hay alguna excursión en barco? — *iy algoona exkoorsyon en barko*

- **How long is the cruise?** — ¿Cuánto dura el crucero? — *kwanto doora el kroothero*

- **Is there wheelchair access?** — ¿Hay acceso para sillas de ruedas? — *iy aktheso para seelyas de rwedas*

- **What is the sea like today?** — ¿Cómo está el mar hoy? — *komo esta el mar oy*

- **Can I/we go out on deck?** — ¿Puedo/Podemos salir a cubierta? — *pwedo/podemos saleer a koobyerta*

YOU MAY HEAR...

- Los barcos salen... los martes y los viernes en días alternos — *los barkos salen... los martes y los byernes en deeas alternos* — Boats go on... Tuesdays and Fridays every other day

- El mar está... en calma picado — *el mar esta... en kalma peekado* — The sea is... calm choppy

✳ air travel
(see **information and tickets**, page 43)

(see **information and tickets**, page 43)

YOU MAY SEE...

Abróchense los cinturones	Fasten seatbelts
Aduana	Customs
Aeropuerto	Airport
Alquiler de coches	Car hire
Cambio	Bureau de change
Control de pasaportes	Passport control
Embarque	Boarding
Facturación	Check-in
Llegadas	Arrivals
Mantengan tus pertenencias controladas en todo momento	Do not leave luggage unattended
Puerta de embarque	Boarding gate
Recogida de equipajes	Luggage reclaim
Retraso	Delay
Sala de embarque	Departure lounge
Salidas	Departures
Seguridad	Security

YOU MAY WANT TO SAY...

- I want to change/ cancel my ticket.

  Quiero cambiar/ cancelar mi billete.

  kyero kambyar kanthelar mee beelyete

- What time do I have to check in?

  ¿A qué hora tengo que facturar?

  a ke ora tengo ke faktoorar

travel and transport

51

Is there a delay?	¿Hay algún retraso?	*iy al**goon** re**tra**so*
Which gate is it?	¿Qué puerta es?	*ke **pwer**ta es*
Have you got a wheelchair?	¿Tienen sillas de ruedas?	*ty**e**nen **see**lyas de **rwe**das*
My luggage hasn't arrived.	Mi equipaje no ha llegado.	*mee ekee**pahhe** no a lye**ga**do*
Is there a bus/ train to the centre (of town)?	¿Hay un autobús/ tren al centro (de la ciudad)?	*iy oon owto**boos**/ tren al **then**tro (de la thyoo**dad**)*

WORDS TO LISTEN OUT FOR...

llamada	*lya**ma**da*	call
vuelo	***bwe**lo*	flight
puerta de embarque	***pwer**ta de em**bar**ke*	gate
última llamada	*ool**tee**ma lya**ma**da*	last call
retraso	*re**tra**so*	delay
cancelado	*kanthe**la**do*	cancelled

✳ taxis
(see **directions**, page 39)

● You can hail taxis in the street, or find them at a taxi rank – look for a sign with a white T on a dark blue background. Taxis that are free have the sign LIBRE.

YOU MAY WANT TO SAY...

Is there a taxi rank round here?	¿Hay alguna parada de taxis por aquí?	*iy al**goo**na pa**ra**da de **tax**ees por a**kee***

● **Can you order me a taxi?**	¿Me puede pedir un taxi?	*me pwede pedeer oon taxee*
● **To this address, please.**	A esta dirección, por favor.	*a esta deerekthyon, por fabor*
● **How much will it cost?**	¿Cuánto costará?	*kwanto kostara*
● **Can you put on the meter?**	¿Puede poner el taxímetro?	*pwede poner el taxeemetro*
● **I'm in a hurry.**	Tengo prisa.	*tengo preesa*
● **Stop here, please.**	Pare aquí (por favor).	*pare akee (por fabor)*
● **Can you wait for me, please?**	¿Puede esperarme?	*pwede esperarme*
● **I think there's a mistake.**	Creo que hay un error.	*kreo ke iy oon error*
● **Keep the change.**	Déjelo así.	*dejelo asee*
● **Can you give me a receipt?**	¿Me puede dar un recibo?	*me pwede dar oon retheebo?*

YOU MAY HEAR...

● Está a diez kilómetros.	*esta a dyeth keelometros*	It's ten kilometres away.
● Hay un suplemento...	*iy oon sooplemento...*	There's a supplement...
por equipaje	*por ekeepahhe*	for the luggage
por cada maleta	*por kada maleta*	for each suitcase
por viajes al aeropuerto	*por byahhes al aeropwerto*	for the journey to the airport

travel and transport

53

✱ hiring cars and bicycles

- I'd like to hire...

  Me gustaría alquilar...

  me goostareea alkeelar...

  - two bicycles

    dos bicicletas

    dos beetheekletas

  - a small car

    un coche pequeño

    oon koche pekenyo

  - an automatic car

    un coche automático

    oon koche owtomateeko

- For one day.

  Para un día.

  para oon deea

- For...

  Durante...

  doorante...

  - a week

    una semana

    oona semana

  - two weeks

    dos semanas

    dos semanas

- How much is it...

  ¿Cuánto cuesta...

  kwanto kwesta...

  - per day?

    al día?

    al deea

  - per week?

    a la semana?

    a la semana

- Is kilometrage included?

  ¿Incluye el kilometraje?

  eenklooye el keelometrahhe

- Is insurance included?

  ¿Incluye el seguro?

  eenklooye el segooro

- My partner wants to drive too.

  Mi pareja también quiere conducir.

  mee parehha tambyen kyere kondootheer

- Do you take...

  ¿Aceptan...

  atheptan...

  - credit cards?

    tarjetas de crédito?

    tarhhetas de kredeeto

  - traveller's cheques?

    cheques de viaje?

    chekes de byahhe

YOU MAY HEAR...

¿Qué tipo de coche/bicicleta desea?	*ke teepo de koche/beetheekleta desea*	**What kind of car/bicycle do you want?**
¿Durante cuánto tiempo?	*doorante kwanto tyempo*	**For how long?**
Su permiso de conducir, por favor.	*soo permeeso de kondootheer, por fabor*	**Your driving licence, please.**
Hay un depósito de 100 euros.	*iy oon deposeeto de thyen eooros*	**There's a deposit of 100 euros.**
¿Tiene una tarjeta de crédito?	*tyene oona tarhheta de kredeeto*	**Have you got a credit card?**
Devuelva el coche con el depósito lleno.	*debwelba el koche kon el deposeeto lyeno*	**Please return the car with a full tank.**
Devuelva el coche/bicicleta antes de las seis.	*debwelba el koche/beetheekleta antes de las says*	**Please return the car/bicycle before six o'clock.**

✳ driving
(see **directions**, page 39)

You drive on the right in Spain, and traffic from the right generally has priority on roads. Seatbelts are compulsory. Crash helmets are compulsory for both drivers and passengers of motorbikes and scooters.

● Speed limits are generally: 50km per hour in towns, 90 or 100km per hour on ordinary roads, and 120km per hour on motorways.

● Main roads are labelled as follows:

A (Autopista) Motorway

N (Carretera Nacional) National highway (those numbered with Roman numberals, e.g. N-IV, start from Madrid)

C (Carretera Comarcal) Provincial or secondary road

YOU MAY SEE...

Alquiler de coches	Car hire
Alto	Stop
Apague el motor	Switch your engine off
Aparcamiento (vigilado/subterráneo)	(Supervised/Underground) car park
Atención	Caution
Autopista (de peaje)	(Toll) motorway
Callejón sin salida	No through road
Carretera cerrada	Road closed
Ceda el paso	Give way
Centro urbano/ciudad	Town/City centre
Circule por la derecha	Keep right
Cuidado	Take care
Curva peligrosa	Dangerous bend
Despacio	Slow
Desviación/Desvío	Diversion
Dirección prohibida	No entry
Dirección única	One-way street
Encender las luces (en túnel)	Use headlights (in tunnel)

Estación de servicio/ gasolinera	Service/petrol station
Estacionamiento (prohibido/ reglamentado)	Parking (prohibited/limited)
Final de autopista	End of motorway
Modere su velocidad	Drive slowly
Obras	Road works
Peatones	Pedestrians
Peligro	Danger
Prioridad a la derecha	Priority to the right
Prohibido adelantar	No overtaking
Prohibido el paso	No entry
Puesto de socorro	First-aid post
Salida	Exit
Uso obligatorio del cinturón de seguridad	Seatbelt compulsory

YOU MAY WANT TO SAY...

- **Where is the nearest petrol station?** ¿Dónde queda la gasolinera más cercana? *donde keda la gasoleenera mas therkana*

- **Fill it up with...** Llénelo con... *lyenelo kon...*
  unleaded gasolina sin plomo *gasoleena seen plomo*
  diesel diésel *dyesel*

- **20 litres of super unleaded, please.** veinte litros de súper sin plomo, por favor. *baynte leetros de sooper seen plomo por fabor*

mechanical problems

A can of oil, please.	Una lata de aceite, por favor.	*oona lata de athayte, por fabor*
Can you check the tyre pressure, please?	¿Puede comprobar la presión de los neumáticos?	*pwede komprobar la presyon de los neoomateekos*
Can you change the tyre, please?	¿Puede cambiar el neumático?	*pwede kambyar el neoomateeko*

* mechanical problems

My car has broken down.	Mi coche se ha estropeado.	*mee koche se a estropeado*
I've run out of petrol.	Me he quedado sin gasolina.	*me e kedado seen gasoleena*
I have a puncture.	Tengo un pinchazo.	*tengo oon peenchatho*
Do you do repairs?	¿Hacen reparaciones?	*athen reparathyones*
I don't know what's wrong.	No sé lo que pasa.	*no se lo ke pasa*
I think it's the...	Creo que es el...	*kreo ke es el...*
I need a...	Necesito un/una...	*netheseeto oon/ oona...*
The ... doesn't work.	El/La ... no funciona.	*el/la ... no foonthyona*
Is it serious?	¿Es algo importante?	*es algo eemportante*

• **Can you repair it today?**	¿Puede repararlo hoy?	*pwede repararlo oy*
• **When will it be ready?**	¿Cuándo estará listo?	*kwando estara leesto*
• **How much will it cost?**	¿Cuánto costará?	*kwanto kostara*

YOU MAY HEAR...

• No tengo los repuestos necesarios.	*no tengo los repwestos nethesaryos*	I don't have the necessary parts.
• Estará listo... a las cuatro el lunes	*estara leesto... a las kwatro el loones*	It'll be ready... at four o'clock on Monday
• Le costará cien euros.	*le kostara thyen eooros*	It'll cost a hundred euros.

✳ car parts

YOU MAY WANT TO SAY...

distributor	el distribuidor	*el deestreebweedor*
engine	el motor	*el motor*
exhaust pipe	el tubo de escape	*el toobo de eskape*
fanbelt	la correa del ventilador	*la korrea del benteelador*
fuel gauge	el indicador de nivel	*el eendeekador de neebel*

travel and transport

gears	las marchas	*las marchas*
gear box	la caja de cambios	*la kahha de kambyos*
headlights	los faros	*los faros*
ignition	el encendido	*el enthendeedo*
indicator	el intermitente	*el eentermeetente*
points	los contactos	*los kontaktos*
radiator	el radiador	*el radyador*
rear lights	las luces traseras	*las loothes traseras*
reversing lights	las luces de marcha atrás	*las loothes de marcha atras*
spare wheel	la rueda de recambio	*rweda de rekambyo*
spark plugs	las bujías	*boohheeas*
starter motor	el motor de arranque	*el motor de arranke*
steering wheel	el volante	*el bolante*
front tyre	la rueda delantera	*la rweda delantera*
back tyre	la rueda trasera	*la rweda trasera*
window	la ventanilla	*la bentaneelya*
windscreen	el parabrisas	*el parabreesas*
windscreen wiper	el limpiaparabrisas	*el leempya-parabreesas*

accommodation

Hotels (hotel – H) are graded from one to five stars according to facilities. Hotel residencias (HR) are also graded but do not have a restaurant. Other types of hotels include apart-hotels (hotel apartamento – HA), and those on the roadside (Hotel de carretera or Motel (M)).

The hostal (Hs) and pensión (P) are more modest guest houses. An hostal residencia (HsR) generally provides a room only (with no meals, not even breakfast).

Cheaper still are the one or two-star fonda (F) and casa de huéspedes (CH), and you will sometimes see signs in bars or outside houses advertising rooms (habitaciones) or beds (camas).

Youth hostels are albergues de juventud and in the mountains you will find refugios (mountain shelters).

YOU MAY SEE...	👁
Agua potable	Drinking water
Albergue de juventud	Youth Hostel
Alojamiento y desayuno	Bed and Breakfast
Ascensor	Lift
Aseos/Baños	Toilets
Basura	Rubbish
Camas	Beds
Camping	Campsite
Casa de huéspedes (CH)	Guest House
Comedor	Dining room

accommodation

Completo	No vacancies
Corriente eléctrica	Electricity
Duchas	Showers
Habitaciones (libres)	Rooms (vacant)
Hostal (Hs)	Hotel, Guest House
Hostal Residencia (HsR)	Hotel, Guest House (no restaurant)
Hotel de cinco estrellas	Five-star hotel
Hotel Residencia (HR)	Hotel (no restaurant)
Lavabos	Toilets
Lavandería	Laundry
Llamar al timbre	Please ring the bell
Media pensión	Half board
Parador	State-owned luxury hotel
Pensión (P)	Boarding-house
Pensión completa	Full board
1er piso/2° piso	First floor/Second floor
Planta baja	Ground floor
Prohibido acampar	No camping
Prohibido hacer fuego	Do not light fires
Recepción	Reception
Refugio	Mountain shelter
Sala de televisión	Television room
Salida (de emergencia)	(Emergency) Exit
Salón	Lounge
Servicio de habitación	Room service
Servicios	Toilets
Tarifa	Charge, tariff

✳ booking in advance
(see telephones, page 132; the internet, page 135)

Many of the larger hotels now have online booking facilities, and you can make your reservations by email.

YOU MAY WANT TO SAY...

- Do you have a ... room?
  - single
  - double
  - family
  - twin-bedded

  ¿Tiene una habitación...
  - individual?
  - doble?
  - familiar?
  - de dos camas?

  tyene oona abeetathyon...
  - *eendeebeedwal*
  - *doble*
  - *fameelyar*
  - *de dos kamas*

- Is breakfast included?

  ¿Se incluye el desayuno?

  se eenklooye el desiyoono

- Do you have...
  - space for a tent?
  - space for a caravan?

  ¿Tiene...
  - sitio para una tienda?
  - sitio para una caravana?

  tyene...
  - *seetyo para oona tyenda*
  - *seetyo para oona karabana*

- I'd like to rent...
  - an apartment
  - a house

  Quiero alquilar...
  - un apartamento
  - una casa

  kyero alkeelar...
  - *oon apartamento*
  - *oona kasa*

- For...
  - one night
  - two nights
  - a week

  Durante...
  - una noche
  - dos noches
  - una semana

  doorante...
  - *oona noche*
  - *dos noches*
  - *oona semana*

- from ... to...

  del ... al...

  del ... al...

- with bath/shower

  con baño/ducha

  kon banyo/doocha

- It's a two-person tent.
  Es una tienda para dos personas.
  es oona tyenda para dos personas

- How much is it...
  ¿Cuánto cuesta...
  kwanto kwesta...
    - per night?
      por noche?
      por noche
    - per week?
      a la semana?
      a la semana

- Is there...
  ¿Hay...
  iy...
    - a reduction for children?
      algún descuento para niños?
      algoon deskwento para neenyos
    - a single room supplement?
      algún recargo por habitación individual?
      algoon rekargo por abeetathyon eendeebeedwal
    - wheelchair access?
      acceso para sillas de ruedas?
      aktheso para seelyas de rwedas

- Can I pay by...
  ¿Puedo pagar con...
  pwedo pagar kon...
    - credit card?
      tarjeta de crédito?
      tarhheta de kredeeto
    - traveller's cheques?
      cheques de viaje?
      chekes de byahhe

- Can I book online?
  ¿Puedo reservar a través de internet?
  pwedo reserbar a trabes de eenternet

- What's the address?
  ¿Cuál es la dirección?
  kwal es la deerekthyon

- Can you recommend anywhere else?
  ¿Puede recomendarme otro sitio?
  pwede rekomendarme otro seetyo

YOU MAY HEAR...

- ¿Durante cuántas noches?
  doorante kwantas noches
  For how many nights?

¿Para cuántas personas?	*para kwantas personas*	For how many people?
¿Una habitación individual o doble?	*oona abeetathyon eendeebeedwal o doble*	Single or double room?
¿Desea una cama matrimonial?	*desea oona kama matreemonyal*	Do you want a double bed?
¿Con baño/ducha?	*kon banyo/doocha*	With bath/shower?
¿Su nombre, por favor?	*soo nombre, por fabor*	What's your name, please?
Lo siento, está completo.	*lo syento, esta kompleto*	I'm sorry, we're full.

✳ checking in

YOU MAY WANT TO SAY...

I have a reservation for...	Tengo una reserva para...	*tengo oona reserba para...*
tonight	esta noche	*esta noche*
two nights	dos noches	*dos noches*
a week	una semana	*oona semana*
It's in the name of...	Está a nombre de...	*esta a nombre de...*
Here's my passport.	Aquí tiene mi pasaporte.	*akee tyene mee pasaporte*

YOU MAY HEAR...

¿Cómo va a pagar?	*komo ba a pagar*	How are you going to pay?

hotels, B&Bs and hostels

¿Ha reservado una habitación/ un sitio?	*a reserbado oona abeetathyon/oon seetyo*	**Have you reserved a room/space?**
¿Me puede dar su pasaporte, por favor?	*me pwede dar soo pasaporte, por fabor*	**Can I have your passport, please?**

REGISTRATION CARD INFORMATION

Nombre	First name
Apellido(s)	Surname(s)
Domicilio/Calle/Nº	Home address/Street/Number
Código postal	Postcode
Nacionalidad	Nationality
Profesión	Occupation
Fecha de nacimiento	Date of birth
Lugar de nacimiento	Place of birth
Número de pasaporte	Passport number
Emitido en	Issued in
Viene de	Coming from
Va a	Going to
Fecha	Date
Firma	Signature

✱ hotels, B&Bs and hostels

YOU MAY WANT TO SAY...

Where can I/we park?	¿Dónde puedo/ podemos aparcar?	*donde pwedo/ podemos aparkar*

accommodation

67

- **Can I/we see the room please?**
  ¿Puedo/podemos ver la habitación, por favor?
  pwedo/podemos ber la abeetathyon, por fabor

- **Do you have...**
  ¿Tiene...
  tyene...
  - **a room with a view?**
    una habitación con vistas?
    oona abeetathyon kon beestas
  - **a bigger room?**
    una habitación mayor?
    oona abeetathyon miyor
  - **a cot for the baby?**
    una cuna para el bebé?
    oona koona para el bebe

- **Is breakfast included?**
  ¿Se incluye el desayuno?
  se eenklooye el desayoono

- **What time...**
  ¿A qué hora...
  a ke ora...
  - **is breakfast?**
    es el desayuno?
    es el desiyoono
  - **do you lock the doors?**
    se cierran las puertas?
    se thyerran las pwertas

- **Where is...**
  ¿Dónde está...
  donde esta...
  - **the dining room?**
    el comedor?
    el komedor
  - **the bar?**
    el bar?
    el bar

- **Is there...**
  ¿Hay...
  iy...
  - **24 hour room service?**
    servicio de habitaciones las veinticuatro horas?
    serbeethyo de abeetathyones las baynteekwatro oras
  - **internet connection?**
    servicio de internet?
    serbeethyo de eenternet
  - **a conference room here?**
    un salón de actos?
    oon salon de aktos

YOU MAY HEAR...

El desayuno está/ no está incluido.	*el desiyoono esta/no esta eenklooweedo*	Breakfast is/isn't included.
El desayuno es de las ... a las...	*el desiyoono es de las ... a las...*	Breakfast is from ... to...
Las puertas se cierran a las...	*las pwertas se thyerran a las...*	We lock the doors at...
El servicio de habitaciones funciona de las ... a las	*el serbeethyo de abeetathyones foonthyona de las ... a las...*	There's room service from ... to...

✳ camping and caravanning
(see **directions**, page 39)

YOU MAY WANT TO SAY...

Is there a campsite round here?	¿Hay un camping por aquí?	*iy oon kampin por akee*
Can we camp here?	¿Podemos acampar aquí?	*podemos akampar akee*
Can we park our caravan here?	¿Podemos acampar aquí con la caravana?	*podemos akampar akee kon la karabana*
It's a two/four person tent.	Es una tienda de dos/ cuatro personas.	*es oona tyenda de dos/kwatro personas*
Where are... the toilets? the showers? the dustbins?	¿Dónde están... los servicios? las duchas? los cubos de la basura?	*donde estan... los serbeethyos las doochas los koobos de la basoora*

69

camping and caravanning

- **Do we pay extra for the showers?** ¿Hay que pagar extra para utilizar las duchas? *iy ke pagar extra para ooteeleethar las doochas*

- **Do I need to use tokens for the showers?** ¿Necesito utilizar fichas para las duchas? *netheseeto ooteeleethar feechas para las doochas*

- **Is the water okay for drinking?** ¿Se puede beber el agua? *se pwede beber el agwa*

- **Where's there an electric point?** ¿Dónde hay un enchufe? *donde iy oon enchoofe*

YOU MAY HEAR... ②

- El camping más cercano está a ... kilómetros. *el kampin mas therkano esta a ... keelometros* The nearest campsite is ... kilometres away.

- Aquí no puede acampar. *akee no pwede akampar* You can't camp here.

- Las duchas son gratuitas. *las doochas son gratweetas* The showers are free.

- Son ... euros por una ducha. *son ... eooros por oona doocha* It's ... euros for a shower.

- Necesita una ficha para tomar una ducha. *netheseeta oona feecha para tomar oona doocha* You need a token to take a shower.

- El enchufe está allí. *el enchoofe esta alyee* The electric point is over there.

accommodation

* requests and queries

- Are there any messages for me?
  ¿Hay algún recado para mí?
  iy algoon rekado para mee

- I'm expecting...
  Estoy esperando...
  estoy esperando...
  - a phone call
    una llamada
    oona lyamada
  - a fax
    un fax
    oon fax

- Can I...
  ¿Puedo...
  pwedo...
  - leave this in the safe?
    dejar esto en la caja fuerte?
    dehhar esto en la kahha fwerte
  - put it on my room bill?
    cargarlo a mi habitación?
    kargarlo a mee abeetathyon

- Can you...
  ¿Podría...
  podreea...
  - give me my things from the safe?
    darme las cosas que tengo en la caja fuerte?
    darme las kosas ke tengo en la kahha fwerte
  - wake me up at eight o'clock?
    despertarme a las ocho en punto?
    despertarme a las ocho en poonto
  - order me a taxi?
    pedirme un taxi?
    pedeerme oon taxee

- Do you have...
  ¿Tienen...
  tyenen...
  - a babysitting service?
    servicio de niñera?
    serbeethyo de neenyera
  - a baby alarm?
    un interfono para bebés?
    oon eenterfono para bebes

- I need...
  Necesito...
  netheseeto...
  - another pillow
    otra almohada
    otra almoada
  - an adaptor
    un adaptador
    oon adaptador

- I've lost my key.
  He perdido la llave.
  e perdeedo la lyabe

I've left my key in the room.	Me he dejado la llave en la habitación.	*me e dehhado la lyabe en la abeetathyon*

* problems and complaints

Excuse me.	Perdone.	*perdone*
The room is...	En la habitación hace...	*en la abeetathyon athe...*
too hot	demasiado calor	*demasyado kalor*
too cold	demasiado frío	*demasyado freeo*
The room is...	La habitación es...	*la abeetathyon es...*
too small/noisy	demasiado pequeña/ruidosa	*demasyado pekenya/rweedosa*
There isn't any...	No hay...	*no iy...*
toilet paper	papel higiénico	*papel eehhyeneeko*
hot water	agua caliente	*agwa kalyente*
electricity	luz	*looth*
There aren't any...	No hay...	*no iy...*
towels	toallas	*toalyas*
soap	jabón	*hhabon*
I can't...	No puedo...	*no pwedo...*
open the window	abrir la ventana	*abreer la bentana*
turn the tap off	cerrar el grifo	*therrar el greefo*
switch on the TV	encender el televisor	*enthender el telebeesor*
The bed is uncomfortable.	La cama es incómoda.	*la kama es eenkomoda*

accommodation

The bathroom is dirty.	El baño está sucio.	*el banyo esta soothyo*
The toilet doesn't flush.	La cisterna no funciona.	*la theesterna no foonthyona*
The washbasin is blocked.	El lavabo está atascado.	*el lababo esta ataskado*
The light/key doesn't work.	La luz/llave no funciona.	*la looth/lyabe no foonthyona*
The shower is not working.	La ducha no funciona.	*la doocha no foonthyona*
There's a smell of gas.	Huele a gas.	*wele a gas*
I want to see the manager!	¡Quiero ver al gerente!	*kyero ber al hherente*

✱ checking out

YOU MAY WANT TO SAY...

The bill, please.	La cuenta, por favor.	*la kwenta, por fabor*
I'd like to... pay the bill and check out stay another night	Quiero... pagar la cuenta para irme quedarme otra noche	*kyero... pagar la kwenta para eerme kedarme otra noche*
What time is check out?	¿A qué hora hay que dejar la habitación?	*a ke ora iy ke dehhar la abeetathyon*

accommodation

73

- Can I...
  leave my
  luggage here?

  ¿Puedo...
  dejar aquí mi
  equipaje?

  pwedo...
  dehhar akee mee
  ekeepahhe

- There's a mistake
  in the bill.

  Hay un error en la
  cuenta.

  iy oon error en la
  kwenta

- I/We've had a
  great time here.

  Me lo he/Nos lo
  hemos pasado muy
  bien aquí.

  me lo e/nos lo emos
  pasado mwee byen
  akee

YOU MAY HEAR...

- Tiene que dejar la
  habitación a las...

  tyene que dehhar
  la abeetathyon a las...

  Check out is at...

- Puede quedarse
  en la habitación
  hasta las...

  pwede kedarse en la
  abeetathyon
  asta las...

  You can have
  the room till...

- ¿Cuántas maletas?

  kwantas maletas

  How many bags?

- Déjelas aquí.

  dehhelas akee

  Leave them here.

- Déjeme ver.

  dehheme ber

  Let me check it.

- ¡Vuelvan por aquí!

  bwelban por akee

  Come again!

✳ self-catering/second homes
(see problems and complaints, page 72)

YOU MAY WANT TO SAY...

- I've rented...
  a villa
  an apartment

  He alquilado...
  una casa
  un apartamento

  e alkeelado...
  oona kasa
  oon apartamento

My name is...	Me llamo...	*me lyamo...*
We're in number...	Estamos en el número...	*estamos en el noomero...*
Can you give me the key, please?	¿Me puede dar la llave, por favor?	*me pwede dar la lyabe, por fabor*
Where is... the fusebox?	¿Dónde está... la caja de fusibles?	*donde esta... la kahha de fooseebles*
the stopcock?	la llave de paso?	*la lyabe de paso*
How does the ... work?	¿Cómo funciona ...?	*komo foonthyona...*
Is there... air-conditioning?	¿Hay... aire acondicionado?	*iy... iyre akondeethyonado*
another gas bottle?	otra bombona de gas?	*otra bombona de gas*
Are there... any more blankets?	¿Hay... más mantas?	*iy... mas mantas*
any shops round here?	alguna tienda cerca de aquí?	*algoona tyenda therka de akee*
Where do I put the rubbish?	¿Dónde pongo la basura?	*donde pongo la basoora*
When do they collect the rubbish?	¿Cuándo pasan a recoger la basura?	*kwando pasan a rekohher la basoora*
When do they come to clean?	¿Cuándo vienen a limpiar?	*kwando byenen a leempyar*

self-catering/second homes

- **Can I borrow...**   ¿Me puede dejar...   *me pwede dehhar...*
  - **a drill?**   un taladro?   *oon taladro*
  - **a corkscrew?**   un sacacorchos?   *oon sakakorchos*
  - **a hammer?**   un martillo?   *oon marteelyo*

- **We need...**   Necesitamos...   *netheseetamos...*
  - **a plumber**   un fontanero   *oon fontanero*
  - **an electrician**   un electricista   *oon elektreetheesta*
  - **help**   ayuda   *iyooda*

- **How can I contact you?**   ¿Cómo puedo ponerme en contacto con usted?   *komo pwedo ponerme en kontakto kon oosteth*

YOU MAY HEAR...

- Funciona así.   *foonthyona asee*   It works like this.

- Déle a este botón/ interruptor.   *dele a este boton/ eenterrooptor*   Press this button/ switch.

- Ponga la basura...   *ponga la basoora*   Put the rubbish...
  - en el contenedor   en el kontenedor   in the dustbin
  - en la calle   en la kalye   on the street

- La basura se recoge los...   *la basoora se rekohhe los...*   The rubbish is collected on...

- Vienen a limpiar los...   *byenen a leempyar los...*   The cleaner comes on...

- Mi número de móvil es el...   *mee noomero de mobil es el...*   My mobile number is...

food&drink

Meal times in Spain are later than in Britain, though restaurants in tourist areas may open earlier. Lunchtime is around 2pm or later, and dinner/supper not before 8.30pm and usually later – around 10 or 10.30pm (later still in areas where there are lots of late-night bars and pubs). Spaniards often have bar snacks (tapas) earlier in the evening and before lunch.

● Almost all bars will serve some snacks and/or sandwiches. During the week, as well as *à la carte*, many restaurants serve a menú del día (set menu) for lunch, offering great value for three courses plus bread and wine.

YOU MAY SEE...

Aceptamos tarjetas de crédito	We take credit cards
Autoservicio	Self-service
Barbacoa/Parrilla	Barbecue/Grill
Bebidas y refrescos	Alcoholic and soft drinks
Bodega	Wine cellar
Cafetería	Café
Cervecería	Pub
Cocina	Kitchen
Comedor	Dining room
Guardarropa	Cloakroom
Heladería	Ice-cream parlour
Marisquería	Seafood restaurant
Menú del día/Menú turístico	Set menu
Merendero	Outdoor bar, picnic area

Platos combinados	Set dishes
Restaurante	Restaurant
Servicios	Toilets
Terraza	Area outdoors with tables

* making bookings
(see **telling the time**, page 17)

(see **telling the time**, page 17)

YOU MAY WANT TO SAY...

- I'd like to reserve a table for... — Quisiera reservar una mesa para... — *kee**sy**era reser**bar** **oo**na **me**sa **pa**ra...*
  - two people — dos personas — *dos per**so**nas*
  - tomorrow evening — mañana por la noche — *man**ya**na por la **no**che*
  - at half past eight — las ocho y media — *las **o**cho ee **me**dya*
  - this evening at nine o'clock — esta noche a las nueve — *esta **no**che a las **nwe**be*

- My name is... — Me llamo... — *me **lya**mo...*

- My telephone/ mobile number is... — Mi número de teléfono/móvil es el... — *mee **noo**mero de te**le**fono/**mo**beel es el...*

- Could you get us a table... — ¿Nos podría conseguir una mesa... — *nos po**dree**a konse**geer oo**na **me**sa...*
  - earlier? — más temprano? — *mas tem**pra**no*
  - later? — más tarde? — *mas **tar**de*

food and drink

YOU MAY HEAR...

¿Para cuándo quiere la mesa?	*para kwando kyere la mesa*	When would you like the table for?
¿Para cuántas personas?	*para kwantas personas*	For how many people?
¿Cómo se llama?	*komo se lyama*	What's your name?
Lo siento, está todo reservado...	*lo syento, esta todo reserbado*	I'm sorry we're fully booked.

✳ at the restaurant

YOU MAY WANT TO SAY...

I've booked a table.	Tengo una mesa reservada.	*tengo oona mesa reserbada*
My name is...	Me llamo...	*me lyamo...*
We haven't booked.	No hemos reservado.	*no emos reserbado*
Have you got a table for four?	¿Tiene mesa para cuatro?	*tyene mesa para kwatro*
Outside/on the terrace, if possible.	Fuera/En la terraza, si fuese posible.	*fwera/en la terratha, si fwese poseeble*
Have you got a high chair?	¿Tienen una silla alta para niños?	*tyenen oona seelya alta para neenyos*
How long's the wait?	¿Cuánto hay que esperar?	*kwanto iy ke esperar*
Do you take credit cards?	¿Aceptan tarjetas de crédito?	*atheptan tarhhetas de kredeeto*

food and drink

YOU MAY HEAR...

¿Tienen una reserva?	*tyenen oona reserba*	Have you got a reservation?
¿Dónde quieren sentarse?	*donde kyeren sentarse*	Where would you like to sit?
¿Fumadores o no fumadores?	*foomadores o no foomadores*	Smoking or non-smoking?
Un momento, por favor.	*oon momento, por fabor*	Just a moment, please.
¿Quieren esperar?	*kyeren esperar*	Would you like to wait?
(No) aceptamos tarjetas de crédito.	*(no) atheptamos tarhhetas de kredeeto*	We (don't) accept credit cards.

* ordering your food

YOU MAY WANT TO SAY...

Excuse me!	¡Perdone!	*perdone*
The menu, please.	¿Me trae la carta?	*me trae la karta*
Do you have... a children's menu? vegetarian food? a set menu?	¿Tienen... menú especial para niños? comida vegetariana? menú del día?	*tyenen... menoo espethyal para neenyos komeeda behhetaryana menoo del deea*
Is it self-service?	¿Es autoservicio?	*es owtoserbeethyo*

• We're ready to order.	Estamos listos para pedir.	*estamos leestos para pedeer*
• Can I have...?	¿Me puede traer...?	*me pwede traer...*
• I'd like...	Quiero...	*kyero...*
for starters	de primer plato	*de preemer plato*
for the main course	de segundo plato	*de segoondo plato*
for dessert	de postre	*de postre*
• Does that come with vegetables?	¿Viene con verdura?	*byene kon berdoora*
• What's this please?	¿Qué es eso?	*ke es eso*
• What are today's specials?	¿Cuáles son los platos del día?	*kwales son los platos del deea*
• What's the local speciality?	¿Cuál es la especialidad local?	*kwal es la espethyalidad lokal*
• I'll have the same as him/her/them.	Para mí lo mismo que él/ella/ellos.	*para mee lo meesmo ke el/elya/elyos*
• I'd like it rare/ medium/well done, please.	Me gusta poco/ medio/bien hecho, por favor.	*me goosta poko/ medyo/byen echo, por fabor*
• Excuse me, I've changed my mind.	Perdone, he cambiado de opinión.	*perdone, e kambyado de opeenyon*

YOU MAY HEAR...   ?

• ¿Están listos?	*estan leestos*	Are you ready to order?

food and drink

82

¿Qué desean de...	ke desean de...	What would you like for...
primer plato?	preemer plato	starters?
segundo plato?	segoondo plato	the main course?
postre?	postre	dessert?
Recomendamos...	rekomendamos...	We recommend...
¿Algo más?	algo mas	Anything else?

* ordering your drinks

Can we see the wine list, please?	¿Podemos ver la carta de vinos, (por favor)?	podemos ber la karta de beenos, (por fabor)
A bottle of this, please.	Una botella de éste, por favor.	oona botelya de este, por fabor
Half a litre of this, please.	Medio litro de éste, por favor.	medyo leetro de este, por fabor
A glass of the ... please.	Un vaso del ... por favor.	oon baso del ... por fabor
We'll have the house red/white, please.	El vino tinto/blanco de la casa, por favor.	el beeno teento/blanko de la kasa, por fabor
What beers do you have?	¿Qué cervezas tienen?	ke therbethas tyenen
Is that a bottle or draught?	¿Es en botellín o de barril?	es en botelyeen o de barreel

● What wines do you have?	¿Qué vinos tienen?	*ke **beenos tyenen***
● Is there a local wine?	¿Hay algún vino del país?	*ay al**goon beeno** del pa**ees***
● Can I have...	¿Me puede poner...	*me **pwede** poner...*
a gin and tonic?	un gin tonic?	*oon jeen **toneek***
a whisky?	un whisky?	*oon **weeskee***
a vodka and Coke?	un vodka con Coca Cola?	*oon **bodka** kon **koka kola***
● Do you have any liqueurs?	¿Tienen licores?	*tyenen lee**kores***
● A bottle of mineral water, please.	Una botella de agua mineral, por favor.	***oona** bo**telya** de **agwa** mee**neral**, por fa**bor***
● What soft drinks do you have?	¿Qué refrescos tienen?	*ke re**freskos tyenen***

YOU MAY HEAR...

● ¿Con hielo y limón?	*kon **yelo** ee lee**mon***	Ice and lemon?
● ¿Quiere agua también?	*kyere **agwa** tam**byen***	Would you like water as well?
● ¿Con gas o sin gas?	*kon gas o seen gas*	Fizzy or still water?
● ¿Una botella grande o pequeña?	*oona bo**telya grande** o pe**kenya***	A large or small bottle?

food and drink

✶ bars, cafés and tapas

- I'll have... | Me pone... | *me pone...*
  - a coffee | un café | *oon kafe*
  - a white coffee | un café con leche | *oon kafe kon leche*
  - a black coffee | un café solo | *oon kafe solo*
  - a cup of tea | un té | *oon te*
  - ...please | ...por favor | *...por fabor*

- with milk/lemon | con leche/limón | *kon leche/leemon*

- A glass of... | Un vaso de... | *oon baso de...*
  - tap water | agua del grifo | *agwa del greefo*
  - wine | vino | *beeno*

- No ice, thanks. | Sin hielo, gracias. | *seen yelo, grathyas*

- A bottle of water, please. | Una botella de agua, por favor. | *oona botelya de agwa por fabor*

- A piece of... | Un trozo de... | *oon trotho de...*

- A portion of ... please. | Una ración de ... por favor. | *oona rathyon de ... por fabor*

- A slice of... | Una lonja de... | *oona lonhha de...*

- What kind of ... do you have? | ¿Qué ... tienen? | *ke ... tyenen*

- Is there any... | ¿Tiene... | *tyene...*
  - tomato ketchup? | ketchup? | *kechoop*
  - pepper and salt? | pimienta y sal? | *peemyenta ee sal*

- It's my round. | Esta ronda la pago yo. | *esta ronda la pago yo*

- How much is that? | ¿Cuánto es? | *kwanto es*

YOU MAY HEAR...

¿Qué desea?	*ke desea*	What would you like?
¿Grande o pequeño/a?	*grande o pekenyo/a*	Large or small?
¿Con gas o sin gas?	*kon gas o seen gas*	Fizzy or still?
¿Con hielo?	*con yelo*	With ice?

✳ comments and requests

YOU MAY WANT TO SAY...

This is delicious!	¡Está muy rico!	*esta mwee reeko*
Can I have more ... please?	¿Me puede traer más ... por favor?	*me pwede traer mas ... por fabor*
bread	pan	*pan*
water	agua	*agwa*
Can I have ... please?	¿Me puede traer ... por favor?	*me pwede traer ... por fabor?*
a knife	un cuchillo	*oon coocheelyo*
a fork	un tenedor	*oon tenedor*
a spoon	una cuchara	*oona cuchara*
a napkin	una servilleta	*oona serbeelyeta*
another glass	otro vaso	*otro baso*
another bottle of wine	otra botella de vino	*otra botelya de beeno*
I can't eat another thing.	No puedo comer nada más.	*no pwedo komer nada mas*

* special requirements

- I'm diabetic. | Soy diabético/a. | *soy dyabeteeko/a*

- I'm allergic to... | Soy alérgico/a... | *soy alerhheeko/a a...*
  - nuts | los frutos secos | *los frootos sekos*
  - cow's milk | la leche de vaca | *la leche de baka*
  - MSG | al glutamato monosódico | *al glootamato monosodeeko*
  - shellfish | al marisco | *al mareesko*

- I'm vegetarian. | Soy vegetariano/a. | *soy behhetaryano/a*

- I don't eat either meat or fish. | No como ni carne ni pescado. | *no komo nee karne nee peskado*

- I'm vegan. | Soy vegano/a. | *soy begano/a*

- I don't eat any animal product. | No como ningún producto animal. | *no komo neengoon prodookto aneemal*

- I can't eat... | No puedo tomar... | *no pwedo tomar...*
  - dairy products | productos lácteos | *prodooktos lakteos*
  - wheat products | productos derivados del trigo | *prodooktos dereebados del treego*

- Do you have ... food? | ¿Tienen comida... | *tyenen komeeda...*
  - halal | halal? | *alal*
  - kosher | kosher? | *kosher*
  - free-range | ecológica? | *ekolohheeka*
  - low sodium | baja en sodio? | *bahha en sodyo*
  - low fat | baja en grasas? | *bahha en grasas*
  - organic | orgánica? | *organeeka*

food and drink

87

Is that cooked with...	¿Se ha cocinado con...	*se a kotheenado kon...*
butter?	mantequilla?	*mantekeelya*
garlic?	ajo?	*ahho*
nuts?	frutos secos?	*frootos sekos*

YOU MAY HEAR...

Preguntaré en la cocina.	*pregoontare en la kotheena*	I'll check with the kitchen.
Todo lleva...	*todo lyeba...*	It's all got ... in it.
mantequilla	*mantekeelya*	butter
ajo	*ahho*	garlic
frutos secos	*frootos sekos*	nuts

* problems and complaints

YOU MAY WANT TO SAY...

Excuse me.	Perdone.	*perdone*
This is...	Está...	*esta...*
cold	frío/a	*freeo/a*
underdone	poco hecho	*poko echo*
burnt	quemado/a	*kemado/a*
I didn't order this.	No he pedido esto.	*no e pedeedo esto*
I ordered the...	Pedí...	*pedee...*
Is our food coming soon?	¿Tardará mucho nuestra comida?	*tardara moocho nwestra komeeda*

✶ paying the bill

- **The bill, please.** La cuenta, por favor. *la kwenta, por fabor*

- **Is service included?** ¿Está incluido el servicio? *esta eenklweedo el serbeethyo*

- **There's a mistake here.** Hay un error. *iy oon error*

- **That was fantastic, thank you.** Fue estupendo, gracias. *fwe estoopendo, grathyas*

- El servicio no está incluido. *el serbeethyo no esta eenklweedo* Service isn't included.

- Lo siento, sólo aceptamos pagos en efectivo. *lo syento, solo atheptamos pagos en efekteebo* Sorry, we only accept cash.

✶ buying food

- **I'd like...** Quisiera... *keesyera...*
  some of that un poco de eso *oon poko de eso*
  a kilo (of...) un kilo (de...) *oon keelo (de...)*
  half a kilo (of...) medio kilo (de...) *medyo keelo (de...)*
  two hundred grammes of... doscientos gramos de... *dosthyentos gramos de...*
  a piece of that un trozo de eso *oon trotho de eso*

food and drink

● What's that, please?	¿Qué es eso?	*ke es eso*
● How much is...	¿Cúanto cuesta...	*kwanto kwesta...*
that?	eso?	*eso*
a kilo of cheese?	un kilo de queso?	*oon keelo de keso*
● Have you got...	¿Tienen...	*tyenen...*
any bread?	pan?	*pan*
any more?	más?	*mas*
● A bit more/less, please.	Un poco más/menos, por favor.	*oon poko mas/menos por fabor*
● That's enough, thank you.	Vale así, gracias.	*bale asee, grathyas*
● That's all, thank you.	Eso es todo, gracias.	*eso es todo, grathyas*
● I'm looking for the ... section.	Estoy buscando la sección de...	*estoy booskando la sekthyon de...*
frozen food	congelados	*konhhelados*
dairy	productos lácteos	*prodooktos lakteos*
fruit and vegetable	frutas y verduras	*frootas ee berdooras*
● Can I have a bag please?	¿Me puede dar una bolsa, por favor?	*me pwede dar oona bolsa, por fabor*

food and drink

menu reader

DRINKS

agua mineral (con gas/sin gas) mineral water (fizzy/still)

aguardiente strong spirit

amontillado medium dry sherry

anís aniseed liqueur

batido milkshake

botella bottle

brandy brandy

café coffee

   bombón with condensed milk

   con hielo iced

   con leche white

   cortado with a dash of milk

   descafeinado decaffeinated

   solo black

caña a glass of draught beer

cava Spanish sparkling wine (similar to champagne)

cerveza beer

   de barril draught

   en botellín bottled

   negra dark

   sin alcohol alcohol-free

clara shandy

con crianza aged

coñac cognac, brandy

copa glass

cosecha vintage

cubalibre rum and Coke

champán champagne

chocolate (caliente/frío) chocolate (hot/cold)

cóctel cocktail

DO = denominación de origen guarantee of origin and quality of a wine

dulce sweet

embotellado por bottled by

espumoso sparkling

fino light dry sherry

gaseosa soda

gin, ginebra gin

gin tonic gin and tonic

granizado crushed iced drink

hielo ice

horchata de chufas groundnut milk

infusión herbal tea

   de manzanilla camomile

   de menta mint

jarra jug, pitcher

jerez sherry

jugo juice

leche (caliente/fría) milk (hot/cold)

limonada lemonade

manzanilla dry sherry; camomile tea

marca brand

mosto grape juice

naranjada orangeade

oloroso strong, dark sherry

oporto port

Reserva, Gran Reserva wine which has been aged

ron rum

sangría fruit, wine and brandy punch

seco dry

semiseco medium dry

sidra cider

sifón soda; draft beer

soda soda

sol y sombra brandy and aniseed liqueur mixed together

té **tea**
  con leche/limón with milk/lemon
  helado **iced**
tinto de verano **red wine and**
  lemonade with ice
tónica **tonic**
vaso **glass**
vendimia **harvest**
vermut, vermú **vermouth**
vino **wine**
  blanco **white**
  clarete **claret**
  de Jerez **sherry**
  de la casa **house wine**
  de la tierra **superior table wine**
  del país **local wine**

de mesa **table wine**
dulce **sweet**
joven **young (less than a year)**
moscatel **sweet wine from**
  moscatel grapes
rosado **rosé**
seco **dry**
tinto **red**
vodka **vodka**
whisky (con soda) **whisky (with soda)**
zumo **juice**
  de melocotón/limón/naranja
  peach/lemon/orange
  de pera/piña/tomate
  pear/pineapple/tomato

FOOD

A

aceitunas **olives**
  negras/verdes/rellenas (de anchoa)
  black/green/stuffed (with
  anchovies)
acelgas **chard**
adobado/a **marinated**
agridulce **sweet and sour**
aguacate **avocado**
ahumado/a **smoked**
ajillo **garlic and oil**
ajo **garlic**
  blanco **garlic and almond soup**
albaricoque **apricot**
albóndigas **meatballs**
alcachofas **artichokes**
alcaparras **capers**
alioli **garlic mayonnaise**
almejas **clams**
almendras **almonds**

almíbar **syrup**
almuerzo **lunch**
alubias **beans**
  blancas **butter beans**
  pintas **red kidney beans**
ancas de rana **frogs' legs**
anchoas **anchovies**
anguila **eel**
angulas **baby eels**
apio **celery**
arenque **herring**
arroz **rice**
  a la cubana **boiled, with tomato**
  sauce and fried egg
  blanco **boiled**
  con leche **pudding**
asado/a **roast**
atún **tuna**
ave(s) **chicken**
avellanas **hazelnuts**

B

bacalao salted cod
  fresco fresh cod
  a la vizcaína Basque style, with
    peppers, ham, onions, garlic and
    chilli pepper
berenjena aubergine
berza cabbage
besugo sea-bream
bistec steak
bizcocho sponge cake
bocadillo sandwich
bogavante lobster
bollo bread roll
bonito tuna
boquerones fresh anchovies
brasa, a la brasa grilled
brazo de gitano kind of Swiss roll
brocheta kebab
buñuelo light fried pastry (like fritter
  or doughnut)
butifarra white sausage from Catalonia

C

caballa mackerel
cabrito kid
cacahuetes peanuts
calabacín courgette
calabaza marrow
calamares squid
  a la romana deep-fried in batter
caldereta stew
caldo clear soup
  gallego with vegetables, beans
    and pork
callos tripe
  a la madrileña Madrid-style, in a
    spicy sausage and tomato sauce
camarones baby prawns
canelones cannelloni
cangrejo (de río) (river) crab
caracoles snails

carne meat
casa: de la casa of the house
castaña chestnut
catalana: a la catalana Catalan-style,
  with onion, tomato and herbs
cazuela: a la cazuela casseroled
cebolla onion
cena dinner
centollo spider crab
cerdo pork
cereza cherry
champiñón(es) mushroom
chanquetes fish (like whitebait)
chilindrón: al chilindrón with dried red
  peppers, tomato and ham
chipirones baby squid
chirimoya custard apple
chivo goat
chocolate chocolate
chocos squid
chorizo spicy sausage
chuleta chop
chuletón large chop
churros sticks or rings of batter,
  deep-fried
cigalas crayfish
ciruela plum
ciruela pasa prune
cocido stew
  madrileño Madrid speciality: stew
    served in two courses – soup first,
    then chick-pea, meat and
    vegetable stew afterwards
cocido/a boiled
cocina casera home cooking
coco coconut
cóctel (de gambas/de marisco)
  (prawn/seafood) cocktail
cochinillo asado roast suckling pig
codorniz quail
col cabbage
col lombarda red cabbage

food and drink

coles de Bruselas **brussels sprouts**
coliflor **cauliflower**
comida **lunch**
conejo **rabbit**
consomé **consommé**
  al jerez **with sherry**
  con yema **with egg yolk**
  de ave/pollo **chicken**
copa helada **Ice-cream sundae**
cordero **lamb**
costillas **ribs**
crema (de cebolla/de espárragos/de champiñones) **cream (of onion/asparagus/mushrooms) soup**
a la crema **in cream sauce**
crema catalana **baked custard with caramelised topping**
crocante **ice-cream with chopped nuts**
croquetas **croquettes**
cuajada (con miel) **junket (with honey)**

D

día: del día **of the day**
desayuno **breakfast**
dulce de membrillo **quince jelly**

E

embutidos **cold meats**
empanada **meat or fish pasty**
empanado/a **breaded and fried**
emperador **type of swordfish**
encebollado/a **with onions**
endivias **chicory**
ensaimada **sweet snail-shaped pastry (from Mallorca)**
ensalada **salad**
  mixta/verde **mixed/green**
ensaladilla rusa **Russian salad – vegetables in mayonnaise**
entradas **starters**
entrecot **entrecôte steak**

entremeses (variados) **(mixed) hors d'oeuvres**
escabechado/a; en escabeche **pickled, marinated**
escalope (de ternera) **(veal) escalope**
  a la milanesa **breaded veal escalope with cheese**
escarola **endive**
espadín a la toledana **kebab**
espaguetis **spaghetti**
espárragos **asparagus**
especialidad de la casa **house special**
espinacas **spinach**
estofado/a **stewed**

F

fabada (asturiana) **bean, sausage and black pudding stew (from Asturias)**
faisán **pheasant**
fiambres **assorted cold meats and sausages**
fideos **noodles**
filete **steak**
flan **crème caramel**
frambuesa **raspberry**
fresa, fresón **strawberry**
fresco/a **fresh**
frío/a **cold**
frito/a **fried**
fritura de pescado **mixed fried fish**
fruta del tiempo **seasonal fruit**

G

gallina **chicken**
gallo **John Dory (fish)**
gambas **prawns**
garbanzos **chickpeas**
gazpacho (andaluz) **cold soup made of tomatoes, peppers, cucumber, garlic, olive oil and vinegar**
gratinado/a **with cheese topping**
guisado/a **stewed**

guisantes **peas**
   con jamón **cooked with cured ham**
gusto: a su gusto **to your choice**

H

habas **broad beans**
   con jamón **cooked with cured ham**
habichuelas **haricot beans**
helado mantecado **rich vanilla ice-cream**
helado de nata **plain ice-cream**
helados (variados) **(assorted) ice-creams**
hervido/a **boiled**
hierbas **herbs**
hígado **liver**
higo **fig**
hinojo **fennel**
horno: al horno **baked**
huevas **fish eggs**
huevos **eggs**
   a la flamenca **Andalusian-style:**
   baked with spicy sausage, tomato,
   peas, peppers and asparagus
   a la mimosa **boiled eggs, cut in**
   half and the yolk mixed with ham
   in a bechamel sauce
   al plato/fritos **fried**
   cocidos/duros **hard boiled**
   con mayonesa **egg mayonnaise**
   escalfados **poached**
   pasados por agua **soft-boiled**
   revueltos **scrambled**

I

IVA incluido **VAT inclusive**

J

jabalí **wild boar**
jamón **ham**
   ibérico/de Jabugo/de Trevélez **types**
   of Spanish cured ham
   serrano **like Parma ham**
   York **cooked**

jerez: al jerez **with sherry**
judías **beans**
   blancas **haricot**
   verdes **green/French**

L

lacón **type of cooked pork**
langosta **lobster**
langostino **king prawn**
leche frita **thick slices of custard fried**
   in breadcrumbs
leche merengada **milk and meringue**
   sorbet
lechón **suckling pig**
lechuga **lettuce**
lengua **tongue**
lenguado **sole**
lentejas **lentils**
   aliñadas **with vinaigrette**
   guisadas **stewed**
liebre **hare**
limón **lemon**
lista de precios **price list**
lomo de cerdo **loin of pork**
lomo de merluza **hake steak**
longaniza **spicy sausage**
lubina **sea bass**

M

macarrones (gratinados) **macaroni**
   (cheese)
macedonia de fruta **fruit salad**
mahonesa **mayonnaise**
maíz **sweetcorn**
manos/manitos de cerdo **Pig's trotters**
mantecada **small sponge cake**
mantequilla **butter**
manzana **apple**
   asada **baked**
margarina **margarine**
marinera: a la marinera **in fish or**
   seafood and tomato sauce

food and drink

95

mariscada **mixed shellfish**
mariscos **seafood**
mayonesa **mayonnaise**
mazapán **marzipan**
medallones **small steaks**
mejillones **mussels**
melocotón **peach**
melón **melon**
  con jamón **with cured ham**
membrillo **quince jelly**
menestra de verduras **vegetable soup/stew**
menú del día **set menu/menu of the day**
menú turístico **tourist menu**
merluza **hake**
  a la gallega **with paprika and tomatoes**
  a la cazuela **stewed in a white sauce and garlic**
mermelada **jam**
mero **grouper**
miel **honey**
mixto/a **mixed**
mollejas **sweetbreads**
morcilla **black pudding**
mostaza **mustard**

N

nabo **turnip**
naranja **orange**
nata **cream**
natural: al natural **fresh, raw**
natillas **egg custard**
nueces **walnuts**

O

ostras **oysters**

P

paella (valenciana) **rice with shellfish, chicken, peppers, peas, saffron, etc (a paella is a large flat pan used to cook this dish)**
país: del país **local**

pan **bread**
pan con tomate **Bread toasted and rubbed with garlic and fresh tomato**
pan y vino incluidos **bread and wine included**
panaché de legumbres/verduras **mixed vegetables**
panceta **bacon**
parrilla: a la parrilla **grilled**
parrillada **mixed grill**
pasas **raisins**
pastel **cake**
  de queso **cheesecake**
patatas **potatoes**
  bravas **in spicy tomato sauce**
  fritas **chips, crisps**
  guisadas **stewed**
pato **duck**
pavo **turkey**
pechuga de pollo **chicken breast**
pepinillo **gherkin**
pepino **cucumber**
pera **pear**
  al vino **in red wine**
percebes **barnacles**
perdiz **partridge**
perejil **parsley**
pescadilla **whiting**
pescado **fish**
pescaditos **sprats**
pestiños (con miel) **Anís flavoured sugared fritters (dipped in honey)**
pez espada **swordfish**
picadillo **minced meat or sausage**
pierna (de cordero/chivo) **leg (of lamb/goat)**
pil-pil: al pil-pil **with chillis, garlic and oil**
pimentón **paprika**
pimienta **pepper**
pimientos **peppers**
  verdes/rojos **green/red**
  del piquillo **spicy**

pinchos **snacks**
pinchos morunos **small kebabs**
piña **pineapple**
piñones **pine kernels**
pisto **sautéed mixed vegetables
 – courgettes, tomatoes, onions,
 peppers and aubergines**
plancha: a la plancha **grilled (on a griddle)**
plátano **banana**
plato del día **dish of the day**
platos combinados **set dishes**
platos típicos **typical dishes**
pollo **chicken**
 al ajillo **with garlic and oil**
 a la parrilla **grilled**
 asado **roasted**
 en pepitoria **in a sauce of almonds,
 saffron, sherry and hard-boiled eggs**
potaje **thick vegetable soup**
puerro **leek**
pulpitos **baby octopus**
pulpo **octopus**
 a la gallega **with paprika and olive oil**
puntas de espárragos **asparagus tips**
puré (de patata) **mashed potato**

Q
queso **cheese**
 azul **blue**
 de bola **round, mild cheese (like
 Edam)**
 de Burgos **soft cream cheese from
 Burgos**
 de cabra **goat's cheese**
 de Cabrales **strong blue cheese
 from Asturias**
 de oveja **sheep's cheese**
 del país **local cheese**
 fresco **curd cheese**
 manchego **hard cheese from La
 Mancha, usually sheep's milk**
quisquillas **shrimps**

R
rábano **radish**
rabo de buey **oxtail**
raciones **portions**
rape **angler fish**
raya **skate**
rebozado/a **battered or breaded and fried**
rehogado/a **sautéed**
relleno/a **stuffed**
remolacha **beetroot**
repollo **cabbage**
requesón **curd, cream cheese**
revuelto **scrambled eggs**
 de espárragos/gambas/setas **with
 asparagus/prawns/wild mushrooms**
riñones **kidneys**
rodaballo **turbot**
romana: a la romana **deep-fried in batter**
roscas, rosquillas **sweet round pastries**

S
sal **salt**
salchicha **sausage**
salchichón **salami-type sausage**
salmón (ahumado) **salmon (smoked)**
salmonete **red mullet**
salpicón de mariscos **shellfish with
 vinaigrette**
salsa **sauce**
 alioli **garlic mayonnaise**
 bechamel **béchamel, white**
 blanca **white**
 de tomate **tomato**
 romesca **dried red peppers, almonds
 and garlic**
 verde **green – parsley, onion and garlic**
salteado **sautéed**
sandía **watermelon**
sardinas **sardines**
sepia **cuttlefish**
servicio (no) incluido **service (not)
 included**

sesos **brains**
setas **wild mushrooms**
sobrasada **sausage (from Mallorca)**
solomillo **fillet steak**
de cerdo **pork tenderloin**
sopa **soup**
castellana **vegetable**
de ajo **garlic and bread**
de almendra **almond-based**
de arroz **with rice**
de cocido **with stew**
de picadillo **chicken soup with chopped sausage, egg and noodles**
juliana **vegetable**
sorbete **sorbet**

T

tallarines **tagliatelle**
tapas **snacks**
tarta **cake, tart**
al whisky **whisky-flavoured ice-cream cake**
de almendra **almond**
de manzana **apple**
helada **ice-cream cake**
ternera **veal**
tiempo: del tiempo **seasonal**
tinta: en su tinta **in its own ink (squid, etc.)**
tocin(ill)o de cielo **rich crème caramel**
tocino **bacon**
tomate: con tomate **tomato: with tomato sauce**
torrijas **bread sliced, dipped in beaten egg, fried and rolled in sugar and cinnamon or honey**

tortilla **omelette**
española/de patata **Spanish (potato and onion)**
francesa **plain**
tostadas **toast**
trucha **trout**
trufas **truffles**
turrón **nougat**

U

uvas **grapes**

V

vaca: de vaca **beef**
vainilla **vanilla**
vapor: al vapor **steamed**
variado(s)/a(s) **assorted**
venado **venison**
vieiras **scallops**
vinagreta **vinaigrette**
vinagre: en vinagre **vinegar: pickled**

Y

yemas **dessert of whipped egg yolks, brandy and sugar**
yogur **yoghurt**

Z

zanahoria **carrot**
zarzuela de (pescados y) mariscos **spicy (fish and) seafood stew**

sightseeing
&activities

✷ at the tourist office

YOU MAY SEE...

Abierto	Open
Billetes de tren/autobús/ barco	Train/bus/boat tickets
Cerrado	Closed
Folletos	Leaflets
Hoteles	Hotels
Información turística	Tourist information
Mapas/planos	Maps

YOU MAY WANT TO SAY...

- **Do you speak English?** ¿Habla inglés? *abla eengles*

- **Do you have...** ¿Tiene... *tyene...*
  a map of the town? un plano de la ciudad? *oon plano de la thyoodad*
  a list of hotels? una lista de hoteles? *oona leesta de oteles*

- **Can you recommend a...** ¿Puede recomendar un... *pwede rekomendar oon...*
  cheap hotel? hotel barato? *otel barato*
  good campsite? buen camping? *bwen kampeen*

- **Do you have information...** ¿Tiene información... *tyene eenformathyon...*
  in English? en inglés? *en eengles*
  about opening times? sobre los horarios? *sobre los orareeos*

sightseeing and activities

100

- **Can you book...** ¿Puede reservarme... *pwede reserbarme...*
  a hotel room una habitación de *oona abeetathyon*
  for me? hotel? *de otel*
  this day trip esta excursión? *esta exkoorsyon*
  for me?

- **Where is...** ¿Dónde está... *donde esta...*
  the old town? el casco antiguo? *el kasko anteegwo*
  the art la galería *la galereea*
  gallery? de arte? *de arte*
  the ... museum? el museo de...? *el mooseo de...*

- **Is there...** ¿Hay... *iy...*
  a swimming una piscina? *oona peestheena*
  pool?
  a bank? un banco? *oon banko*

- **Is there a post** ¿Hay una oficina *iy oona ofeetheena*
  office near here? de correos cerca de *de korreos therka*
  aquí? *de akee*

- **Can you show** ¿Me lo puede señalar *me lo pwede senyalar*
  me on the map? en el mapa? *en el mapa*

✳ opening times
(see **telling the time**, page 17)

YOU MAY WANT TO SAY...

- **What time does** ¿A qué hora abre *a ke ora abre el*
  the museum/ el museo/palacio? *mooseo/palathyo*
  palace open?

- **What time** ¿A qué hora cierra la *a ke ora thyerra la*
  does the church/ iglesia/catedral? *eegleseea/katedral*
  cathedral close?

● **When does the exhibition open?**	¿Cuándo abre la exposición?	*kwando abre la exposee***thyon**
● **Is it open...**	¿Está abierto...	*esta abyerto...*
on Mondays?	los lunes?	*los loones*
at the weekend?	los fines de semana?	*los feenes de semana*
● **Can I/we visit...**	¿Puedo/podemos visitar...	*pwedo/podemos bisitar...*
the monastery?	el monasterio?	*el monastereeo*
● **Is it open to the public?**	¿Está abierto al público?	*esta abyerto al poobleeko*

YOU MAY HEAR...

● Abre todos los días excepto...	*abre todos los deeas exthepto*	It's open every day except...
● Abre de ... a...	*abre de ... a...*	It's open from... to...
● Está cerrado los...	*esta therrado los...*	It's closed on...
● Está cerrado durante el invierno.	*esta therrado doorante el eenbyerno*	It's closed in winter.

✳ visiting places

YOU MAY SEE...

Abierto	Open
Cerrado (por reparaciones)	Closed (for restoration)
Horario de visitas	Opening hours

visiting places

No pisar el césped	Keep off the grass
No tocar	Do not touch
Prohibida la entrada	No entry
Prohibido sacar fotografías con flash	No flash photography
Privado	Private
Visitas con guía	Guided tours

YOU MAY WANT TO SAY...

- **How much does it cost to get in?** — ¿Cuánto cuesta entrar? — *kwanto kwesta entrar*

- **Two adults, please.** — Dos adultos, por favor. — *dos adooltos, por fabor*

- **One adult and two children, please.** — Un adulto y dos niños, por favor. — *oon adoolto y dos neenyos, por fabor*

- **A family ticket, please.** — Un billete familiar, por favor. — *oon beelyete fameelyar, por fabor*

- **Is there a reduction for...** — ¿Hay algún descuento para... — *iy algoon deskwento para...*
    - **students?** — estudiantes? — *estoodyantes*
    - **pensioners?** — jubilados? — *hhoobeelados*
    - **children?** — niños? — *neenyos*

visiting places

- **Is there...**
  wheelchair access?
  ¿Hay... acceso para sillas de ruedas?
  iy... aktheso para seelyas de rwedas

  an audio tour? audioguías? *owdyogeeas*

- **Are there guided tours (in English)?** ¿Hay visitas guiadas (en inglés)? *iy beeseetas geeadas (en eengles)*

- **Can I take photos?** ¿Puedo sacar fotos? *pwedo sakar fotos*

- **Can you take a photo of us?** ¿Nos puede sacar una foto? *nos pwede sakar oona foto*

- **When was this built?** ¿Cuándo se construyó? *kwando se konstrooyo*

- **Who painted that?** ¿Quién lo pintó? *kyen lo peento*

- **How old is it?** ¿Cuántos años tiene? *kwantos anyos tyene*

YOU MAY HEAR...

- Cuesta ... euros por persona.
  kwesta ... eooros por persona
  It costs ... euros per person.

- Hay un descuento para estudiantes/ personas mayores.
  iy oon deskwento para estoodyantes/ personas miyores
  There's a reduction for students/senior citizens.

- Los niños menores de ... entran gratis.
  los neenyos menores de ... entran gratees
  Children under ... go free.

- Hay rampas para sillas de ruedas.
  iy rampas para seelyas de rwedas
  There are wheelchair ramps.

sightseeing and activities

* going on tours and trips

I'd like to join the tour to...	Me gustaría apuntarme a la excursión a...	me goostareea apoontarme a la exkoorsyon a...
What time does it...	¿A qué hora...	a ke ora...
leave?	sale?	sale
get back?	vuelve?	bwelbe
How long is it?	¿Cuánto dura?	kwanto doora
Where does it leave from?	¿De dónde sale?	de donde sale
Does the guide speak English?	¿Habla el guía inglés?	abla el geea eengles
How much is it (per day)?	¿Cuánto cuesta (al día)?	kwanto kwesta (al deea)
Is lunch/ accommodation included?	¿Incluye el alojamiento/la comida?	eenklooye el alohhamyento/la komeeda
When's the next...	¿Cuándo es la próxima...	kwando es la prokseema...
boat trip?	excursión en barco?	exkoorsyon en barko
day trip?	excursión de un día?	exkoorsyon de oon deea
Can we hire...	¿Podemos alquilar...	podemos alkeelar...
a guide?	un guía?	oon geea
an English-speaking guide?	un guía que hable inglés?	oon geea ke able eengles

105

- **I'm with a group.** Estoy con un grupo. *estoy* kon oon **groo**po

- **I've lost my group.** He perdido a mi grupo. e per**dee**do a mee **groo**po

YOU MAY HEAR...

Sale a las...	*sale* a las...	It leaves at...
Vuelve a...	**bwelbe** a...	It gets back at...
Sale de...	*sale* de...	It leaves from...
(Él/Ella) cobra... al día.	*(el/elya) kobra ... al **deea**	He/She charges ... per day.
¿Cómo se llama su grupo?	*komo* se **lyama** soo **groo**po	What's the name of your group?

* entertainment

● Evening performances at theatres, cinemas, musical events, flamenco shows etc. often start late – around 10.30 or 11pm, and may require booking in advance. Spaniards often don't go out until 10 or 11pm, and many bars and clubs stay open until the early hours.

YOU MAY SEE...

Agotado	Sold out
Anfiteatro	Amphitheatre, Circle (in theatre)

Butacas (de patio)	Seats (in the stalls)
Cine	Cinema
Discoteca	Nightclub
Estadio	Stadium
Fila	Row
Guardarropa	Cloakroom
Hipódromo	Racecourse
Localidades para hoy	Tickets for today's performance
Mayores de 13/18 años	Over 13s/18s only
No hay descanso	There is no interval
No recomendada para menores de 13/18 años	Not recommended for under 13s/18s
No se permite la entrada una vez comenzado el espectáculo	No entry once the performance has begun
Palcos	Boxes
Patio de butacas	Stalls
Sala de conciertos	Concert hall
Salón de baile	Dance hall
Sesión continua	Continuous performance
Sesión de noche	Evening performance
Sesión de tarde	Matinée
Teatro	Theatre
Teatro de la ópera	Opera house
Todos los públicos	For general viewing
Venta anticipada	Advance booking
Versión original subtitulada (v.o.)	Original language version with subtitles

sightseeing and activities

sightseeing and activities

YOU MAY WANT TO SAY...

- **Is there anything for children?** ¿Hay algo para los niños? *iy algo para los neenyos*

- **Is there ... round here?** ¿Hay ... por aquí? *iy ... por akee*
  - **a cinema** un cine *oon theene*
  - **a nightclub** una discoteca *oona deeskoteka*

- **What's on...** ¿Qué ponen... *ke ponen...*
  - **tonight?** esta noche? *esta noche*
  - **tomorrow?** mañana? *manyana*
  - **at the theatre?** en el teatro? *en el teatro*
  - **at the cinema?** en el cine? *en el theene*

- **When does the game/performance start?** ¿Cuándo comienza el partido/el espectáculo? *kwando komyentha el parteedo/ espektacoolo*

- **What time does it finish?** ¿A qué hora acaba? *a ke ora akaba*

- **How long is it?** ¿Cuánto dura? *kwanto doora*

- **Do we need to book?** ¿Hay que reservar entradas? *iy ke reserbar entradas*

- **Where can I/we get tickets?** ¿Dónde se puede conseguir entradas? *donde se pwede konsegeer entradas*

- **Is it suitable for children?** ¿Es apto para niños? *es apto para neenyos*

- **Has the film got subtitles?** ¿Es una película subtitulada? *es oona peleekoola soobteetoolada*

- **Is it dubbed?** ¿Está doblada? *esta doblada*

YOU MAY HEAR...

Aquí puede comprar entradas.	*akee pwede komprar entradas*	You can buy tickets here.
Empieza a las...	*empyetha a las...*	It starts at...
Acaba a las...	*akaba a las...*	It finishes at...
Es mejor reservar por adelantado.	*es mehhor reserbar por adelantado*	It's best to book in advance.
Está doblada.	*esta doblada*	It's dubbed.
Tiene subtítulos en inglés.	*tyene soobteetoolos en eengles*	It's got English subtitles.

✳ booking tickets

YOU MAY WANT TO SAY...

Can you get me tickets for...	¿Puede conseguirme entradas para...	*pwede konsegeerme entradas para...*
the ballet?	el ballet?	*el balet*
the football match?	el partido de fútbol?	*el parteedo de footbol*
the theatre?	el teatro?	*el teatro*
Are there any seats left for Saturday?	¿Quedan localidades para el sábado?	*kedan lokalidades para el sabado*
I'd like to book...	Quiero reservar...	*kyero reserbar...*
a box	un palco	*oon palko*
two seats	dos localidades	*dos lokaleedades*

booking tickets

● **in the stalls**	en el patio de butacas	*en el patyo de bootakas*
● **in the balcony**	en el anfiteatro	*en el anfeeteatro*
● **in the shade/sun**	de sombra/sol	*de sombra/sol*
● **Do you have anything cheaper?**	¿Tiene algo más barato?	*tyene algo mas barato*
● **Is there wheelchair access?**	¿Hay acceso para sillas de ruedas?	*iy aktheso para seelyas de rwedas*

YOU MAY HEAR...

● ¿Cuántas?	*kwantas*	How many?
● ¿Para cuándo?	*para kwando*	When for?
● ¿Tiene tarjeta de crédito?	*tyene tarhheta de kredeeto*	Do you have a credit card?
● Lo siento pero se han agotado las entradas para ese día/esa noche.	*lo syento pero se an agotado las entradas para ese deea/esa noche*	I'm sorry we're sold out that day/night.

sightseeing and activities

✳ at the show

What film/ play/opera is on tonight?	¿Qué película/ obra/ópera ponen hoy?	ke peleekoola/ obra/opera ponen oy
One adult and two children, please.	Un adulto y dos niños, por favor.	oon adoolto y dos neenyos, por fabor
How much is that?	¿Cuánto es?	kwanto es
We'd like to sit... at the front at the back in the middle	Nos gustaría sentarnos... hacia delante hacia atrás en el medio	nos goostareea sentarnos... athya delante athya atras en el medyo
We've reserved seats.	Tenemos asientos reservados.	tenemos asyentos reserbados
My name is...	Me llamo...	me lyamo...
Is there an interval?	¿Hay descanso?	iy deskanso
Where's... the balcony? the bar?	¿Dónde está... el anfiteatro? el bar?	donde esta... el anfeeteatro el bar
Where are the toilets?	¿Dónde están los servicios?	donde estan los serbeethyos
Can you stop talking, please?!	¿Se podría callar, por favor?	se podreea kalyar, por fabor

sightseeing and activities

111

* sports and activities

YOU MAY SEE...

Alquiler de barcos	Boat hire
Alquiler de esquís	Ski hire
Campo de fútbol	Football pitch
Campo de golf	Golf course
Coto de caza	Hunting reserve
Coto (privado)	(Private) Reserve
Escuela de esquí	Ski school
Peligro	Danger
Piscina (cubierta)	(Indoor) Swimming pool
Pista	Ski slope
Pista de tenis	Tennis court
Playa	Beach
Polideportivo	Sports Centre
Prohibido bañarse	No swimming
Prohibido el paso/Propiedad privada	No trespassing/Private property
Prohibido pescar	No fishing
Puesto de socorro	First Aid
Teleférico	Cable Car
Telesilla	Chair lift
Remonte	Ski lift

YOU MAY WANT TO SAY...

- **Where can I/we...** ¿Dónde se puede... *donde se pwede...*
  play tennis? jugar al tenis? *hhoogar al tenees*
  play golf? jugar al golf? *hhogar al golf*

sports and activities

- **Can I/we...** — ¿Se puede... — *se pwede...*
  - go riding? — montar a caballo? — *montar a kabalyo*
  - go fishing? — pescar? — *peskar*
  - go skiing? — esquiar? — *eskyar*
  - go swimming? — nadar? — *nadar*

- **I'm...** — Soy... — *soy...*
  - a beginner — principiante — *preentheepyante*
  - quite experienced — bastante experto/a — *bastante experto/a*

- **How much does it cost...** — ¿Cuánto cuesta... — *kwanto kwesta...*
  - per hour? — a la hora? — *a la ora*
  - per day? — al día? — *al deea*
  - per week? — a la semana? — *a la semana*
  - per round? — por recorrido? — *por recorreedo*
  - per game? — por partida? — *por parteeda*

- **Can I/we hire...** — ¿Se pueden alquilar... — *se pweden alkeelar...*
  - clubs? — los palos? — *los palos*
  - raquets? — las raquetas? — *las raketas*

- **Do you give lessons?** — ¿Dan clases? — *dan klases*

- **Do I/we have to be a member?** — ¿Hay que ser miembro? — *iy ke ser myembro*

- **Can children do it too?** — ¿También lo pueden hacer los niños? — *tambyen lo pweden ather los neenyos*

- **Is there a reduction for children?** — ¿Hay algún descuento para niños? — *iy algoon deskwento para neenyos*

- **What's...** — ¿Cómo está... — *komo esta...*
  - the water like? — el agua? — *el agwa*
  - the snow like? — la nieve? — *la nyebe*

113

at the beach, river or pool

YOU MAY HEAR...

Cuesta ... euros por hora.	*kwesta ... eooros por ora*	It costs ... euros per hour.
Hay un depósito reembolsable de... euros.	*iy oon deposeeto rembolsable de ... eooros*	There's a refundable deposit of ... euros.
En este momento estamos completos.	*en este momento estamos kompletos*	We're full at the moment.
¿Qué talla usa?	*ke talya oosa*	What size are you?
Necesita... una foto seguro	*netheseeta... oona foto segooro*	You need... a photo insurance

* at the beach, river or pool

YOU MAY WANT TO SAY...

Can I/we swim here?	¿Se puede nadar aquí?	*se pwede nadar akee*
Is it dangerous?	¿Es peligroso?	*es peleegroso*
Is it safe for children?	¿Es seguro para los niños?	*es segooro para los neenyos*
When is high tide?	¿Cuándo sube la marea?	*kwando soobe la marea*
Is the water clean?	¿Está limpia el agua?	*esta leempya el agwa*
Where is the lifeguard?	¿Dónde está el socorrista?	*donde esta el sokorreesta*

sightseeing and activities

114

shops&services

✳ shopping

To ask for something in a shop, all you need do is name it and add 'please', por favor *(por fabor)* – or just point and say 'this one here', éste de aquí *(este de akee)*, or 'two of those', dos de ésos *(dos de esos)*.

YOU MAY SEE...

Abierto (todo el día)	Open (all day)
Almacenes	Department store
Alimentación	Groceries
Antigüedades	Antiques
Artículos de cuero/piel	Leather goods
Artículos de deporte	Sports goods
Autoservicio	Self-service
Bodega	Wine cellar
Bricolaje	DIY shop
Buzón	Post box
Caja	Cashier
Calzados	Footwear
Carnicería	Butcher's
Centro comercial	Shopping centre
Cerrado	Closed
Charcutería	Delicatessen
Comestibles	Groceries
Confecciones	Fashions
Confitería	Confectioner's
Correos	Post office

shops and services

116

Discos	Records
Droguería	Drugstore
Electrodomésticos	Electrical goods
Entrada	Entry
Farmacia (de guardia)	(Duty) Chemist's
Ferretería	Hardware store
Flores, Floristería	Flowers, Florist's
Frutas, Frutería	Fruits, Fruit shop
Golosinas	Sweet shop
Joyería	Jeweller's
Juguetes, Juguetería	Toys, Toy shop
Librería	Bookshop
Liquidación	Closing down sale
Moda	Fashion
Muebles, Mueblería	Furniture, Furniture shop
No tocar	Do not touch
Ofertas	Special offers
Óptica	Optician's
Ordenadores	Computers
Panadería	Baker's
Papelería	Stationer's
Pastelería	Cake shop
Peluquería	Hairdresser's
Perfumería	Perfumery
Pescadería	Fishmonger's
Prensa	Newsagent's
Probadores	Fitting rooms
Productos dietéticos	Health foods
PVP (Precio de Venta al Público)	Retail Price

shopping

Spanish	English
Rebajas	Sales
Recuerdos	Souvenirs
Regalos	Gifts
Relojería	Watchmaker's
Ropa (de señoras/de caballeros/infantil)	Clothes (women's/men's/children's)
Salida (de emergencia)	(Emergency) exit
Sótano	Basement
Supermercado	Supermarket
Tabacos	Tobacconist's
Tienda de informática	Computer shop
Tienda de fotografía	Photography shop
Tintorería	Dry-cleaners
Ultramarinos	Groceries
Venta de sellos	Stamps for sale
Verdulería	Greengrocer's
Zapatería	Shoe shop

YOU MAY WANT TO SAY...

- Where is...
  the shopping centre?
  the post office?

  ¿Dónde está...
  el centro comercial?
  el Correos?

  donde esta...
  el thentro komerthyal
  el korreos

- Where can I buy...

  ¿Dónde puedo comprar...

  donde pwedo komprar...

  suntan lotion?
  a map?

  un bronceador?
  un mapa?

  oon brontheador
  oon mapa

shops and services

118

I'd like ... please.	Quiero ... por favor.	*kyero ... por fabor*
that one there	ése de allí	*ese de alyee*
this one here	éste de aquí	*este de akee*
two of those	dos de ésos	*dos de esos*
Have you got... ?	¿Tiene... ?	*tyene...*
How much does it cost?	¿Cuánto cuesta?	*kwanto kwesta*
How much do they cost?	¿Cuánto cuestan?	*kwanto kwestan*
Can you write it down please?	¿Me lo puede escribir?	*me lo pwede eskreebeer*
I'm just looking.	Sólo estoy mirando.	*solo estoy meerando*
There's one in the window.	Hay uno/a en la ventana.	*iy oono/oona en la bentana*
I'll take it.	Me lo llevo.	*me lo lyebo*
Is there a guarantee?	¿Tiene garantía?	*tyene garanteea*
Can you...	¿Me lo puede...	*me lo pwede...*
keep it for me?	guardar?	*gwardar*
order it for me?	pedir?	*pedeer*
I/We need to think about it.	Tengo/Tenemos que pensarlo.	*tengo/tenemos ke pensarlo*

YOU MAY HEAR...

¿En qué puedo ayudarle?	*en ke pwedo iyoodarle*	How can I help you?

shops and services

119

paying

Cuesta ... euros.	*kwesta ... eooros*	It costs ... euros.
Lo siento, se nos ha agotado.	*lo syento, se nos a agotado*	I'm sorry, we've sold out.
Podemos pedirlo para usted.	*podemos pedeerlo para oosteth*	We can order it for you.

* paying

YOU MAY WANT TO SAY...

Where do I pay?	¿Dónde se paga?	*donde se paga*
Do you take credit cards?	¿Aceptan tarjetas de crédito?	*atheptan tarhhetas de kredeeto*
Can you wrap it, please?	¿Puede envolverlo?	*pwede enbolberlo*
Can I have... a receipt? a bag? my change?	¿Me puede dar... un recibo? una bolsa? la vuelta?	*me pwede dar... oon retheebo oona bolsa la bwelta*
Sorry, I haven't got any change.	Lo siento, no tengo suelto.	*lo syento, no tengo swelto*

YOU MAY HEAR...

¿Quiere que se lo envuelva?	*kyere ke se lo enbwelba*	Do you want it wrapped?
¿Cómo desea pagar?	*komo desea pagar*	How do you want to pay?

buying clothes and shoes

¿Me permite...	*me permeete...*	Can I see...
su carné de identidad?	*soo carne de eedenteedad*	some ID, please?
su pasaporte?	*soo pasaporte*	your passport, please?

✳ buying clothes and shoes
(see **conversions**, page 21)

YOU MAY WANT TO SAY...

- **Have you got...** | ¿Tiene... | *tyene...*
  - **the next size up/down?** | una talla más/ menos? | *oona talya mas/ menos*
  - **other colours?** | otros colores? | *otros kolores*

- **What size is this in British sizes?** | ¿A qué talla británica corresponde? | *a ke talya breetaneeka korresponde*

- **I'm size...** | Soy la talla... | *soy la talya...*

- **I'm looking for...** | Estoy buscando... | *estoy booskando...*
  - **a shirt** | una camisa | *oona kameesa*
  - **a pair of jeans** | un par de vaqueros | *oon par de bakeros*
  - **a jumper** | un jersey | *oon hherse-ee*
  - **a jacket** | una chaqueta | *oona chaketa*
  - **a skirt** | una falda | *oona falda*
  - **a t-shirt** | una camiseta | *oona kameeseta*
  - **a hat** | un sombrero | *oon sombrero*

- **A pair of...** | Un par de... | *oon par de...*
  - **trousers** | pantalones | *pantalones*
  - **shoes** | zapatos | *thapatos*
  - **sandals** | sandalias | *sandalyas*
  - **boots** | botas | *botas*

shops and services

121

changing rooms, exchanges

- **Where are the changing rooms?** ¿Dónde están los probadores? *donde estan los probadores*

✳ changing rooms

- **Can I try this on, please?** ¿Me lo puedo probar, por favor? *me lo pwedo probar por fabor*

- **It's too...** Es demasiado... *es demasyado...*
  - **big** grande *grande*
  - **small** pequeño/a *pekenyo/a*

- **It doesn't suit me.** No me queda bien. *no me keda byen*

¿Le gustaría probárselo(s)?	*le goostareea probarselo(s)*	Would you like to try it/them on?
¿Cuál es su talla?	*kwal es soo talya*	What size are you?
Le traigo otro.	*le triygo otro*	I'll get you another one.
Lo siento, es el último que nos queda.	*lo syento, es el oolteemo ke nos keda*	Sorry, that's the last one.

✳ exchanges and refunds

- **This has a flaw.** Esto tiene un defecto. *esto tyene oon defekto*

● Excuse me, this doesn't work.	Perdone, esto no funciona.	*perdone, esto no foonthyona*
● This doesn't fit.	No me queda bien.	*No me keda byen*
● I'd like...	Quiero...	*kyero...*
a refund	que me devuelvan el dinero	*ke me debwelban el deenero*
a new one	otro nuevo	*otro nwebo*
● I'd like...	Quería...	*kereea...*
to return this	devolver esto	*debolber esto*
to change this	descambiar esto	*deskambyar esto*

YOU MAY HEAR...

● ¿Tiene...	*tyene...*	Have you got...
el recibo?	*el retheebo*	the receipt?
la garantía?	*la garanteea*	the guarantee?
● Lo siento pero no devolvemos el dinero.	*lo syento pero no debolbemos el deenero*	Sorry, we don't give refunds.

✳ bargaining

YOU MAY WANT TO SAY...

● Is this your best price?	¿Es éste su mejor precio?	*es este soo mehhor prethyo*
● It's too expensive.	Es demasiado caro/a.	*es demasyado karo/a.*
● Is there a reduction for cash?	¿Hay algún descuento si se paga en efectivo?	*iy algoon deskwento see se paga en efekteebo*

• I'll give you...	Le doy...	*le doy...*
• That's my final offer.	Es mi última oferta.	*es mee ooltima oferta*
• Take it or leave it.	Lo toma o lo deja.	*lo toma o lo dehha*

✳ at the drugstore
(see at the chemist, page 138)

● Although you may find some toiletries and cosmetics at the chemist's, these are usually medicated or for special conditions such as delicate skins or allergies. For toiletries and cosmetics, you need to visit a perfumería or droguería.

YOU MAY WANT TO SAY...

● I need...	Necesito...	*Netheseeto...*
shampoo	champú	*champoo*
shower gel	gel de ducha	*hhel de doocha*
deodorant	desodorante	*desodorante*
moisturising cream	crema hidratante	*krema eedratante*
toothpaste	pasta de dientes	*pasta de dyentes*
tampons	unos tampones	*oonos tampones*
sanitary towels	unas compresas	*oonas kompresas*
toilet paper	papel higiénico	*papel eehhyeneeko*
aftersun	aftersun	*aftersoon*
● I am looking for...	Estoy buscando...	*estoy booskando...*
a perfume	un perfume	*oon perfoome*
a (pink) nail varnish	un esmalte de uñas (rosa)	*oon esmalte de oonyas (rosa)*

shops and services

- I'd like some...   Quisiera un...   *keesyera oon...*
  make-up remover   desmaquillante   *desmakeellante*
  toner   tónico   *toneeko*
  foundation   maquillaje de base *makeelyahhe de base*

* photography

- Can you develop this film for me? | ¿Me puede revelar este carrete? | *me pwede rebelar este karrete*

- I have a digital camera. | Tengo una cámara digital. | *tengo oona kamara deehheetal*

- Can you print photos from a memory card? | ¿Puede imprimir las fotos de una tarjeta de memoria? | *pwede eempreemer las fotos de oona tarhheta de memorya*

- Can you develop this film as slides for me? | ¿Me puede revelar este carrete como diapositivas? | *me pwede rebelar este karrete komo deeaposeeteebas*

- Do you sell imaging software? | ¿Tiene software para restauración de imágenes? | *tyene softwer para restowrathyon de eemahhenes*

- When will it/they be ready? | ¿Cuándo estará/n lista/s? | *kwando estara/n leesta/s*

- Do you have an express service? | ¿Tiene servicio de revelado rápido? | *tyene serbeethyo de rebelado rapeedo*

- Does it cost extra? | ¿Cuesta más? | *kwesta mas*

How much does it cost...	¿Cuánto cuesta...	kwanto kwesta...
per film?	por carrete?	por karrete
per print?	por foto?	por foto

I need...	Necesito...	netheseeto...
a colour film	un carrete en color	oon karrete en kolor
a black and white film	un carrete en blanco y negro	oon karrete en blanko ee negro
a memory card	una tarjeta de memoria	oona tarhheta de memorya

I'd like...	Quiero...	kyero...
a 24 exposure film	un carrete de 24 fotos	oon karrete de baynteekwatro fotos
a 36 exposure film	un carrete de 36 fotos	oon karrete de traynta ee says fotos
a disposable camera	una cámara desechable	oona kamara desechable

My camera is broken.	Mi cámara no funciona.	mee kamara no foonthyona
Do you do repairs?	¿Hacen reparaciones?	athen reparathyones

YOU MAY HEAR...

¿De qué tamaño desea las fotos?	de ke tamanyo desea las fotos	What size do you want your prints?

¿Las quiere mate o con brillo?	*las kyere mate o kon breelyo*	Do you want them matt or gloss?
Vuelva...	*bwelba...*	Come back...
mañana	*manyana*	tomorrow
dentro de una hora	*dentro de oona ora*	in an hour
¿De cuántas fotos lo quiere?	*de kwantas fotos lo kyere*	How many exposures do you want?

✱ at the tobacconist

Cigarettes and tobacco are sold in State-controlled tobacconists (estancos) – they have the sign Tabacos (and a yellow symbol on a brown background). Tobacconists also sell stamps, official documents, phone cards (both for telephone boxes and mobiles) and occasionally bus tickets.

YOU MAY WANT TO SAY...

Can I have a packet of...	¿Me da un paquete de...?	*me da oon pakete de...*
Do you have matches/lighters?	¿Tiene cerillas/ mecheros?	*tyene thereelyas/ mecheros*
Do you have any cigars?	¿Tiene puros?	*tyene pooros*
A stamp for Great Britain please.	Un sello para Gran Bretaña, por favor.	*oon selyo para gran bretanya por fabor*

Five stamps for the USA, please.	Cinco sellos para los Estados Unidos, por favor.	*theenko selyos para los estados ooneedos por fabor*

✳ at the post office

Post offices (Correos) are generally open from 8am to 1 or 1.30pm and 4pm to 6 or 7pm, Mondays to Fridays and Saturday mornings. Letterboxes (buzón) are painted yellow with a red symbol. If you only want stamps, go to a tobacconist (estancos – see page 127) of which there are far more than post offices.

(estancos – see page 127)

YOU MAY WANT TO SAY...

A stamp for Great Britain please.	Un sello para Gran Bretaña, por favor.	*oon selyo para gran bretanya por fabor*
Five stamps for America, please.	Cinco sellos para los Estados Unidos, por favor.	*theenko selyos para los estados ooneedos por fabor*
Can I send this... registered?	¿Puedo enviar esto... por correo certificado?	*pwedo enbeear esto... por korreo therteefeekado*
airmail?	por correo aéreo?	*por korreo aereo*
It contains...	Contiene...	*kontyene...*
Do you change money here?	¿Aquí cambian dinero?	*akee kambyan deenero*
Can I have a receipt?	¿Me puede dar un recibo?	*me pwede dar oon retheebo*

¿Para España o el extranjero?	*para espanya o el extranhhero*	For Spain or abroad?
Póngalo en la báscula, por favor.	*pongalo en la baskoola, por fabor*	Put it on the scales, please.
¿Qué hay dentro?	*ke iy dentro*	What's in it?
Rellene este formulario de declaración de aduana.	*relyene este formoolaryo de deklarathyon de adwana*	Please fill in this customs declaration form.

✳ at the bank

● Banks (Banco) are usually open from 9am to 2pm, Mondays to Fridays, and 9am to 12.30 or 1pm on Saturdays. In summer they may close a bit earlier.

YOU MAY WANT TO SAY...

Excuse me, where's the foreign exchange counter?	Perdone, ¿dónde está el mostrador de cambio de moneda?	*perdone, donde esta el mostrador de kambyo de moneda*
Is there a cashpoint machine here?	¿Tienen cajero automático?	*tyenen cahhero owtomateeko*
The cashpoint machine has eaten my card.	El cajero se ha tragado mi tarjeta.	*el cahhero se a tragado mee tarhheta*
I've forgotten my pin number.	Se me ha olvidado mi número personal.	*se me a olbidado mee noomero personal*

changing money

● Can I check my account, please?	¿Puedo comprobar mi cuenta, por favor?	*pwedo komprobar mee kwenta, por fabor*
● My account number is...	Mi número de cuenta es...	*mee noomero de kwenta es...*
● My name is...	Me llamo...	*me lyamo...*
● I'd like to...	Quiero...	*kyero...*
withdraw some money	sacar dinero	*sakar deenero*
pay some money in	ingresar dinero	*eengresar deenero*
cash this cheque	cobrar este cheque	*kobrar este cheke*
● Has my money arrived yet?	¿Ya ha llegado mi dinero?	*ya a lyegado mee deenero*

YOU MAY HEAR...

● Su carné de identidad, por favor.	*soo karne de eedenteedad, por fabor*	Your ID, please.
● Su pasaporte, por favor.	*soo pasaporte, por fabor*	Your passport, please.
● Su saldo es de...	*soo saldo es de...*	Your balance is...
● Tiene su cuenta al descubierto en ... euros.	*tyene soo kwenta al deskoobyerto en ... eooros*	You're overdrawn by ... euros.

✳ changing money

● The Spanish unit of currency is the euro. There are coins of 1, 2, 5, 10, 20 and 50 cents (céntimos), 1 and 2 euros;

and banknotes of 5, 10, 20, 50, 100, 200 and 500 euros.

YOU MAY WANT TO SAY...

I'd like to change ... please.	Quiero cambiar... por favor.	*kyero kambyar... por fabor*
these travellers' cheques	estos cheques de viaje	*estos chekes de byahhe*
one hundred pounds	cien libras	*thyen leebras*
Can I have... small/new notes?	¿Me puede dar... billetes pequeños nuevos?	*me pwede dar... beelyete pekenyo/ nwebos*
some change?	algo de suelto?	*algo de swelto*
Can I get money out on my credit card?	¿Puedo sacar dinero con mi tarjeta de crédito?	*pwedo sakar deenero kon mee tarhheta de kredeeto*
What's the rate today...	¿Cuál es el tipo de cambio de hoy para...	*kwal es el teepo de kambyo de oy para...*
for the pound?	la libra?	*la leebra*
for the dollar?	el dólar?	*el dolar*
for the euro?	el euro?	*el eooro*

YOU MAY HEAR...

¿Cuánto?	*kwanto*	How much?
Su pasaporte, por favor.	*soo pasaporte, por fabor*	Your passport, please.
Firme aquí.	*feerme akee*	Sign here, please.
Son ... euros por libra.	*son ... eooros por leebra*	It's ... euros to the pound.

✳ telephones

● Public telephones take all euro coins except the 1 cent piece. Most telephones also accept credit cards, while some take either coins or cards. You can buy prepaid phone cards for international calls in estancos (tobacconists) (prices range from 4 to 15 euros).

YOU MAY WANT TO SAY...

● **Where's the (nearest) phone?**
¿Dónde está el teléfono (más cercano)?
donde esta el telefono (mas therkano)

● **Is there a public phone?**
¿Hay un teléfono público?
iy oon telefono poobleeko

● **Have you got change for the phone, please?**
¿Tiene suelto para el teléfono, por favor?
tyene swelto para el telefono, por fabor

● **The number is...**
El número es...
el noomero es...

● **How much does it cost per minute?**
¿Cuánto cuesta por minuto?
kwanto kwesta por meenooto

● **I'd like to...**
Quisiera...
keesyera...
   buy a phone card
   comprar una tarjeta telefónica
   komprar oona tarhheta telefoneeka
   call England
   llamar a Inglaterra
   lyamar a eenglaterra
   make a reverse charge call
   hacer una llamada a cobro revertido
   ather oona lyamada a kobro reberteedo

shops and services

132

What's the area code for...?	¿Cuál es el prefijo local de... ?	*kwal es el prefeehho lokal de...*
What's the country code?	¿Cuál es el prefijo del país?	*kwal es el prefeehho del paees*
How do I get an outside line?	¿Cómo puedo acceder a una línea externa?	*komo pwedo aktheder a oona leenea externa*
Hello.	Diga.	*deega*
It's... speaking.	Soy...	*soy...*
Can I have extension ... please?	¿Me puede poner con la extensión ... por favor?	*me pwede poner kon la extensyon ... por fabor*
Can I speak to... ?	¿Puedo hablar con... ?	*pwedo ablar kon...*
When will he/she be back?	¿Cuándo volverá?	*kwando bolbera*
I'll ring back.	Volveré a llamar.	*bolbere a lyamar*
Can I leave a message?	¿Puedo dejar un recado?	*pwedo dehhar oon rekado*
My number is...	Mi número es...	*mee noomero es...*
Can you say ... called?	¿Puede decirle que ... ha llamado?	*pwede detheerle ke ... a lyamado*
Sorry, I've got the wrong number.	Lo siento, me he equivocado de número.	*lo syento, me e ekeebokado de noomero*
It's a bad line.	La línea está mal.	*la leeneea esta mal*
I've been cut off.	Se ha cortado.	*se a kortado*
They've hung up on me.	Me han colgado.	*me an kolgado*

shops and services

133

mobiles

* mobiles

● If your phone is not barred for international use (check with your service provider before leaving the UK), you should not have any problem using your mobile in Spain. Some UK companies also operate in Spain so you may be able to use your usual service provider. Otherwise your mobile will connect to one of the local networks.

YOU MAY WANT TO SAY...

● Have you got...	¿Tiene...	*tyene...*
a charger for this phone?	un cargador para este móvil?	*oon kargador para este mobil*
a SIM card for the local network?	una tarjeta SIM para la red local?	*oona tarhheta seem para la red lokal*
a pay-as-you-go phone?	un teléfono de tarjeta?	*oon telefono de tarhheta*

Can I hire a mobile?	¿Puedo alquilar un móvil?	*pwedo alkeelar oon mobil*
What's the tariff?	¿Cuál es la tarifa?	*kwal es la tareefa*
Are text messages included?	¿Se incluyen los mensajes de texto?	*se eenklooyen los mensahhes de texto*
How do you make a local call?	¿Cómo se puede hacer una llamada local?	*komo se pwede ather oona lyamada lokal*
Is there a code?	¿Hay un prefijo?	*iy oon prefeehho*
How do you send text messages?	¿Cómo envía los mensajes de texto?	*komo enbeea los mensahhes de texto*
How can I change the ring tone?	¿Cómo puedo cambiar la melodía?	*komo pwedo kambyar la melodeea*

* the internet

Is there an internet cafe near here?	¿Hay un cibercafé cerca de aquí?	*iy oon theeberkafe therka de akee*
I'd like to... log on check my emails	Quisiera... conectarme comprobar mis emails	*keesyera... konektarme komprobar mees eemayls*
How much is it per minute?	¿Cuánto cuesta por minuto?	*kwanto kwesta por meenooto*
I can't log on.	No puedo entrar.	*no pwedo entrar*
It's not connecting.	No se conecta.	*no se konekta*
It's very slow.	Va muy lento.	*ba mwee lento*

faxes

- **Can you...**
  print this?
  scan this?

  ¿Me puede...
  imprimir esto?
  escanear esto?

  me pwede...
  eempreemeer esto
  eskanear esto

- **Can I...**
  run this?
  download this?

  ¿Puedo...
  ejecutar esto?
  descargar esto?

  pwedo...
  ehhecootar esto
  deskargar esto

- **Do you have...**
  a CD-Rom?
  a zip drive?

  a UBS lead?

  ¿Tiene...
  un CD-Rom?
  una unidad zip?

  una conexión
  UBS?

  tyene...
  un thede-rrom
  *oona ooneedad
  theep*
  *oona konexyon
  oo be ese*

YOU MAY SEE...

Nombre de usuario	Username
Contraseña	Password
Haga/Haz clic	Click here
Enlace/Vínculo	Link

✱ faxes

YOU MAY WANT TO SAY...

- **What's your fax
  number?**

  ¿Cuál es su número
  de fax?

  *kwal es soo
  noomero de fax*

- **Can you send this
  fax for me, please?**

  ¿Me puede enviar
  este fax, por favor?

  *me pwede enbyar
  este fax, por fabor*

- **How much is it?**

  ¿Cuánto cuesta?

  kwanto kwesta

health&safety

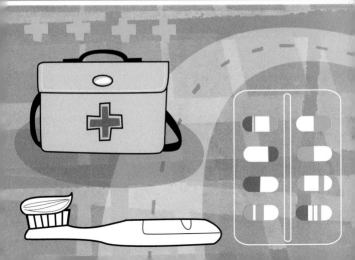

✳ at the chemist's
(see **at the drugstore**, page 124)

● Chemists (farmacia) have a green cross sign outside. They are generally open from 9.30am to 2pm and 4.30pm to 8pm. Chemists sell mainly medicines, baby and health products. For toiletries and cosmetics, go to a perfumería or droguería.

YOU MAY WANT TO SAY...

● **Have you got something for...**	¿Tiene algo para...	*tyene algo para...*
sunburn?	las quemaduras de sol?	*las kemadooras de sol*
diarrhoea?	la diarrea?	*la dyarrea*
period pains?	los dolores menstruales?	*los dolores menstroowales*
headaches?	el dolor de cabeza?	*el dolor de kabetha*
stomach ache?	el dolor de estómago?	*el dolor de estomago*
a sore throat?	el dolor de garganta?	*el dolor de garganta*
● **I need some ... please.**	Necesito ... por favor.	*netheseeto... por fabor*
aspirin	unas aspirinas	*oonas aspeereenas*
plasters	unas tiritas	*oonas teereetas*
painkillers	unos calmantes	*oonos kalmantes*
insect repellent	un repelente de insectos	*oon repelente de eensektos*
suntan lotion	un bronceador	*oon brontheador*
travel sickness pills	unas pastillas para el mareo	*oonas pasteelyas para el mareo*
condoms	unos condones	*oonos kondones*

✳ at the doctor's
(see **medical complaints and conditions**, page 141)

(see **medical complaints and conditions**, page 141)

YOU MAY WANT TO SAY...

- I need a doctor (who speaks English).

  Necesito un médico (que hable inglés).

  netheseeto oon medeeko (ke able eengles)

- Can I make an appointment?

  ¿Puede concertarme una cita?

  pwede conthertarme oona theeta

- I've run out of my medication.

  Me he quedado sin medicamentos.

  me e kedado seen medeekamentos

- I'm on medication for...

  Estoy tomando medicamentos para...

  estoy tomando medeekamentos para...

- I've had a... jab

  Estoy vacunado/a contra...

  estoy bakoonado/a kontra...

  - tetanus
  - typhoid
  - rabies

  - el tétanos
  - la tifoidea
  - la rabia

  - *el tetanos*
  - *la teefoidea*
  - *la rabya*

- I've had a ... vaccination.

  Estoy vacunado/a contra...

  estoy bakoonado/a kontra...

  - polio
  - measles

  - la polio
  - el sarampión

  - *la polyo*
  - *el sarampyon*

- Can I have a receipt for my health insurance, please?

  ¿Me puede dar un recibo para dárselo a mi seguro médico privado, por favor?

  me pwede dar oon retheebo para darselo a mee segooro medeeko preebado, por fabor

health and safety

139

✱ describing your symptoms

● To indicate where the pain is you can simply point and say 'it hurts here' (me duele aquí). Otherwise you'll need to look up the Spanish for the appropriate part of the body.

YOU MAY WANT TO SAY...

● I don't feel well.	No me siento bien.	no me **syen**to byen
● It's my...	Es mi...	es mi...
● It hurts here.	Duele aquí.	**dwe**le a**kee**

● My... hurts.
  stomach
  head
  face
	Me duele...
	  el estómago
	  la cabeza
	  la cara
		me **dwe**le...
		  el es**to**mago
		  la ka**be**tha
		  la **ka**ra

● My... hurt.
  ears
  feet
	Me duelen...
	  los oídos
	  los pies
		me **dwe**len...
		  los o**ee**dos
		  los pyes

● I'm dizzy.	Estoy mareado/a.	es**toy** ma**rea**do/a
● I feel sick.	Tengo ganas de vomitar.	**ten**go **ga**nas de bo**mee**tar

● I can't ...
  breathe properly
  sleep properly
	No puedo ...
	  respirar bien
	  dormir bien
		no **pwe**do...
		  respee**rar** byen
		  dor**meer** byen

● I've cut/burnt myself.	Me he cortado/ quemado.	me e kor**ta**do/ ke**ma**do
● I've been sick.	He estado enfermo/a.	e es**ta**do en**fer**mo/a

* medical complaints and conditions

- I'm...
  asthmatic
  diabetic
  arthritic
  epileptic

  Tengo...
  asma
  diabetes
  artritis
  epilepsia

  tengo...
  asma
  deeabetes
  artreetees
  epeelepsya

- I'm...
  pregnant
  blind
  deaf

  Estoy...
  embarazada
  ciego/a
  sordo/a

  estoy...
  embarathada
  thyego/a
  sordo/a

- I've got...
  high/low blood
    pressure
  a heart
    condition

  Tengo...
  la tensión alta/
    baja
  una enfermedad
    del corazón

  tengo...
  la tensyon alta/
    bahha
  oona enfermedad
    del korathon

- I use a wheelchair.

  Utilizo una silla de
  ruedas

  ooteeleetho oona
  seelya de rwedas

- I have difficulty
  walking.

  tengo problemas de
  mobilidad.

  tengo problemas de
  mobeeleedad

- I'm HIV positive.

  Soy seropositivo.

  soy seroposeeteebo

- I'm allergic to...
  antibiotics
  penicillin
  cortisone

  Tengo alergia a...
  los antibióticos
  la penicilina
  la cortisona

  tengo alerhhya a...
  los anteebyoteekos
  la peneetheeleena
  la korteesona

- I suffer from...
  hay fever
  angina

  Tengo...
  alergia al polen
  angina de pecho

  tengo...
  alerhhya al polen
  anhheena de pecho

health and safety

141

medical complaints and conditions

YOU MAY HEAR...

Spanish	Pronunciation	English
¿Dónde le duele?	*donde le dwele*	Where does it hurt?
¿Está tomando algún medicamento?	*esta tomando algoon medeekamento*	Are you on medication?
¿Tiene algún tipo de alergia?	*tyene algoon teepo de alerhhya*	Are you allergic to anything?
Tengo que tomarle la temperatura.	*tengo ke tomarle la temperatoora*	I need to take your temperature.
Desvístase, por favor.	*desbeestase, por fabor*	Get undressed, please.
Acuéstese aquí, por favor.	*akwestese akee, por fabor*	Lie down here, please.
No es nada grave.	*no es nada grabe*	It's nothing serious.
Tiene una infección.	*tyene oona eenfekthyon*	You've got an infection.
Está infectado/a.	*esta eenfektado/a*	It's infected.
Necesito una muestra de sangre/orina/heces.	*netheseeto oona mwestra de sangre/oreena/ethes*	I need a blood/urine/stool sample.
Necesita hacer una radiografía.	*netheseeta ather oona radyografeea.*	You need an X-ray.
Voy a darle una inyección.	*boy a darle oona eenyekthyon*	I'm going to give you an injection.
Tome esto ... veces al día.	*tome esto ... bethes al deea*	Take this ... times a day.

health and safety

142

Debe descansar.	*debe deskansar*	You must rest.
No debe beber alcohol.	*no debe beber alkol*	You mustn't drink alcohol.
Tiene que ir al hospital.	*tyene ke eer al ospeetal*	You need to go to hospital.
Tiene un esguince en...	*tyene oon esgeenthe en...*	You've sprained your...
Se ha roto...	*se ha roto...*	You've broken your...
Tiene...	*tyene...*	You've got...
gripe	*greepe*	flu
apendicitis	*apendeetheetees*	appendicitis
bronquitis	*bronkeetees*	bronchitis
Es un infarto.	*es oon eenfarto*	It's a heart attack.

✳ parts of the body

YOU MAY WANT TO SAY...

ankle	el tobillo	*tobeelyo*
appendix	el apéndice	*apendeethe*
arm	el brazo	*bratho*
artery	la arteria	*artereea*
back	la espalda	*espalda*
bladder	la vejiga	*behheega*
blood	la sangre	*sangre*
body	el cuerpo	*kwerpo*
bone	el hueso	*weso*
bottom	el trasero	*trasero*
bowels	los intestinos	*eentesteenos*
breast	el pecho	*pecho*

English	Spanish	Pronunciation
buttock	la nalga	*nalga*
cartilage	el cartílago	*karteelago*
chest	el tórax	*torax*
chin	la barbilla	*barbeelya*
collar bone	la clavícula	*klabeekoola*
ear		
(internal)	el oído	*oeedo*
(external)	la oreja	*orehha*
elbow	el codo	*kodo*
eye	el ojo	*ohho*
face	la cara	*kara*
finger	el dedo	*dedo*
foot	el pie	*pye*
genitals	los genitales	*hheneetales*
gland	el ganglio	*ganglyo*
hair	el pelo	*pelo*
hand	la mano	*mano*
head	la cabeza	*kabetha*
heart	el corazón	*korathon*
heel	el talón	*talon*
hip	la cadera	*kadera*
jaw	la mandíbula	*mandeeboola*
joint	la articulación	*arteekoolathyon*
kidney	el riñón	*reenyon*
knee	la rodilla	*rodeelya*
leg	la pierna	*pyerna*
ligament	el ligamento	*leegamento*
lip	el labio	*labyo*
liver	el hígado	*eegado*
lung	el pulmón	*poolmon*
mouth	la boca	*boka*
muscle	el músculo	*mooskoolo*
nail	la uña	*oonya*

neck	el cuello	*kwelyo*
nerve	el nervio	*nerbyo*
nose	la nariz	*nareeth*
penis	el pene	*pene*
rib	la costilla	*kosteelya*
shoulder	el hombro	*ombro*
skin	la piel	*pyel*
spine	la espina dorsal	*espeena dorsal*
stomach	el estómago	*estomago*
tendon	el tendón	*tendon*
testicle	el testículo	*testeekoolo*
thigh	el muslo	*mooslo*
throat	la garganta	*garganta*
thumb	el pulgar	*poolgar*
toe	el dedo del pie	*dedo del pye*
tongue	la lengua	*lengwa*
tonsils	las amígdalas	*ameegdalas*
tooth	el diente	*dyente*
vagina	la vagina	*bahheena*
vein	la vena	*bena*
wrist	la muñeca	*moonyeka*

✳ at the dentist's

YOU MAY WANT TO SAY...

- I've got toothache. / Tengo dolor de muelas. / *tengo dolor de mwelas*

- This tooth (really) hurts. / Me duele (mucho) este diente. / *me dwele(mucho) este dyente*

- It's my wisdom tooth. / Es la muela del juicio. / *es la mwela del hhweethyo*

health and safety

- I've lost... | He perdido... | e perdeedo...
    - a filling | un empaste | oon empaste
    - a crown/cap | una corona/funda | oona korona/foonda

- I've broken a tooth. | Me ha roto un diente. | me a roto oon dyente

- **Can you fix it temporarily?** | ¿Puede arreglarlo temporalmente? | pwede arreglarlo temporalmente

YOU MAY HEAR...

Abra la boca, por favor.	*abra la boka, por fabor*	Open your mouth, please.
Apriete las mandíbulas.	*apryete las mandeeboolas*	Bite your jaws together.
Necesita un empaste.	*netheseeta oon empaste*	You need a filling.
Tengo que sacarlo.	*tengo ke sakarlo*	I'll have to take it out.
Voy a ponerle...	*boy a ponerle...*	I'm going to give you...
una inyección	*oona eenyekthyon*	an injection
un empaste temporal	*oon empaste temporal*	a temporary filling
una corona temporal	*oona korona temporal*	a temporary crown

✳ emergencies

- If you need an ambulance, call the emergency number 112, the police or the Spanish Red Cross, la Cruz Roja, the numbers for which change depending on where you are.

emergencies

YOU MAY SEE...

Agítese antes de usar	Shake before use
Casa/Puesto de socorro	First aid post
Clínica	Hospital
Consulta	Surgery hours
Enfermera	Nurse
Hospital	Hospital
Médico	Doctor
Modo de empleo	Instructions for use
Servicio de urgencias	Emergency services
Sólo para uso externo	For external use only
Urgencias	Casualty department
Veneno	Poison

YOU MAY WANT TO SAY...

- I need...   Necesito...   *netheseeto...*
    - a doctor   a un médico   *oon medeeko*
    - an ambulance   una ambulancia   *oona amboolanthya*
    - the fire brigade   a los bomberos   *a los bomberos*
    - the police   a la policía   *a la poleetheea*

- Immediately!   ¡Inmediatamente!   *eenmedyatamente*

- Help!   ¡Socorro!   *sokorro*

- Please help me.   Ayúdeme por favor.   *iyoodeme por fabor*

- There's a fire.   Hay un incendio.   *iy oon eenthendyo*

- There's been an accident.   Ha habido un accidente.   *a abeedo oon aktheedente*

health and safety

147

I have to use the phone.	Tengo que utilizar el teléfono.	*tengo ke ooteeleethar el telefono*
I'm lost.	Me he perdido.	*me e perdeedo*
I've lost my... son/daughter friends	He perdido a... mi hijo/a mis amigos	*e perdeedo a... mee eehho/a mees ameegos*
Stop!	¡Alto!	*alto*

* police

YOU MAY WANT TO SAY...

Sorry, I didn't realise it was against the law.	Lo siento, no sabía que era ilegal.	*lo syento, no sabeea ke era eelegal*
Here are my documents.	Aquí tiene mi documentación.	*akee tyene mee dokoomentathyon*
I haven't got my passport with me.	No traigo conmigo el pasaporte.	*no tr:ygo konmeego el pasaporte*
I don't understand.	No entiendo.	*no entyendo*
I'm innocent.	Soy inocente.	*soy eenothente*
I need a lawyer (who speaks English).	Necesito un abogado (que hable inglés).	*netheseeto oon abogado (ke able eengles)*
I want to contact my embassy/ consulate.	Quiero ponerme en contacto con mi embajada/consulado.	*kyero ponerme en kontakto con mee embahhada/ konsoolado*

YOU MAY HEAR...

Tendrá que pagar una multa.	*tendra ke pagar oona moolta*	You'll have to pay a fine.
Su documentación por favor.	*soo dokoomentathyon por fabor*	Your documents please.
Queda detenido.	*keda deteneedo*	You're under arrest.

✳ reporting crime

YOU MAY WANT TO SAY...

I want to report a theft.	Quiero denunciar un robo.	*kyero denoonthyar oon rrobo*
My ... has been stolen.	Me han robado...	*me an robado...*
purse	el monedero	*el monedero*
bag	la bolsa	*la bolsa*
wallet	la cartera	*la kartera*
Our car has been broken into.	Nos han entrado a robar en el coche.	*nos an entrado a rrobar en el koche*
I've lost my...	He perdido...	*e perdeedo...*
credit cards	mis tarjetas de crédito	*mees tarhhetas de kredeeto*
suitcase	la maleta	*la maleta*
luggage	mi equipaje	*mee ekeepahhe*
I've been...	Me han...	*me an...*
mugged	robado	*rrobado*
attacked	agredido	*agredeedo*

reporting crime

YOU MAY HEAR...

¿Cuándo ocurrió?	*kwando okoorryo*	When did it happen?
¿Dónde?	*donde*	Where?
¿Qué ocurrió?	*ke okoorryo*	What happened?
Tendrá que rellenar este formulario.	*tendra ke relyenar este formoolaryo*	You'll have to complete this form.
¿Qué aspecto tenía?	*ke aspekto teneea*	What did he/she look like?

YOU MAY WANT TO SAY...

- It happened...
  - five minutes ago
  - last night
  - on the beach

  Ocurrió...
  - hace cinco minutos
  - anoche
  - en la playa

  okoorryo...
  - *athe theenko meenootos*
  - *anoche*
  - *en la pliya*

- He/She had...
  - blonde hair
  - a knife

  Tenía...
  - el pelo rubio
  - un cuchillo

  teneea...
  - *el pelo rroobyo*
  - *oon koocheelyo*

- He/She was...
  - tall
  - short
  - young

  Era...
  - alto/a
  - bajo/a
  - joven

  era...
  - *alto/a*
  - *bahho/a*
  - *hhoben*

- He/She was wearing...
  - jeans
  - a red shirt

  Llevaba...
  - vaqueros
  - una camisa roja

  lyebaba...
  - *bakeros*
  - *oona kameesa rohha*

basic grammar

✴ nouns

All Spanish nouns have a gender – masculine or feminine.
You can often tell the gender from the word ending. Most
nouns ending in -o are masculine. The few exceptions include
mano (hand) and foto (photo). Nouns ending in -or are also
generally masculine.

Most nouns ending in -a are feminine. Exceptions include día
(day), mapa (map), and words ending in -ma like problema
(problem) and clima (climate). Nouns ending in -dad and
-ión are also generally feminine. Words with other endings
can be either gender – the Dictionary indicates which.

A masculine plural noun can refer to a mixture of masculine
and feminine, e.g.
hijos (sons or children, i.e. sons and daughters)
los españoles (Spanish men or the Spanish)

✴ plurals

Nouns are generally made plural by adding s if they end in
a vowel or es if they end in a consonant, e.g.

libro – libros   coche – coches   hotel – hoteles

✴ articles (a, an, the)

The Spanish indefinite article (the equivalent of 'a' or 'an') has
different forms: un is used with masculine nouns, una with
feminine ones, e.g.

un coche   una camisa

The definite article ('the') has different forms for masculine and feminine, and also for singular and plural:

	MASCULINE	FEMININE
singular	el	la
plural	los	las
example:	el coche	la camisa
	los coches	las camisas

In the Dictionary, nouns are marked to show their gender: (m) for masculine and (f) for feminine.

✳ adjectives

Adjectives 'agree' with the nouns they are describing – they have different endings for masculine and feminine, singular and plural.

Many adjectives end in -o for masculine and -a for feminine, with an added s for the plural of both, e.g.

un coche blanco   una camisa blanca
coches blancos   camisas blancas

Some adjectives have only one ending for the singular, both masculine and feminine, and add s or es for the plural. They include those ending in -e and those ending in a consonant, e.g.

un coche verde   una camisa verde
coches verdes   camisas verdes

un coche azul   una camisa azul
coches azules   camisas azules

Note that adjectives denoting a person's nationality, even if they end in a consonant, have different endings for masculine and feminine, e.g.:

	MASCULINE	FEMININE
singular	inglés	inglesa
plural	ingleses	inglesas
singular	español	española
plural	españoles	españolas

✳ position of adjectives

Most adjectives come after the noun,
e.g.:

vino blanco (white wine)
excursiones turísticas (tourist excursions)
una camisa azul (a blue shirt)

Some common adjectives always come before the noun,
including:

bueno (good)	malo (bad)
mucho (much, many)	poco (not much, few)
bastante (quite a lot)	demasiado (too much/many)
alguno (any, some)	otro (other)
todo (every, all)	cada (each)
primero (first)	último (last)

e.g.

otros coches (other cars)
todos los días (every day)
la primera vez (the first time)

✳ comparatives and superlatives

'More' is más and comes before the adjective – it also
gives the equivalent of 'bigger', 'smaller', e.g.:

más interesante (more interesting)
más grande (bigger)
más viejo (older)

'Less' is menos:
menos importante (less important)
menos complicado (less complicated)

The comparatives of 'good' and 'bad' are mejor (better) and peor (worse).

'Than', as in 'more than' and 'less than', is que, e.g. este coche es más grande que el otro (this car is bigger than the other).

To say 'the most' or 'the least', put the definite article el or la before más or menos, e.g.
la región más interesante (the most interesting region)
el/la más grande del mundo (the biggest in the world)

✱ possessives (my, your, his, her, etc.)

Like other adjectives, possessive adjectives 'agree' with the nouns they are describing. The forms are:

	SINGULAR		PLURAL	
	m	f	m	f
my	mi		mis	
your	tu		tus	
his/her/your*	su		sus	
our	nuestro	nuestra	nuestros	nuestras
your	vuestro	vuestra	vuestros	vuestras
their/your*	su		sus	

(* 'Your' when addressing someone as usted – see 'You' page 156.)

mi hermano (my brother)

nuestra casa (our house)

There is no Spanish equivalent of the English apostrophe s as in 'John's brother', 'John and Susan's house', etc. Instead, the word de ('of') is used:

el hermano de John (John's brother)

la casa de John y Susan (John and Susan's house)

✳ demonstratives (this, that)

There is one way of saying 'this' and two of saying 'that' – one for things that are fairly close, the other two for things 'over there':

	SINGULAR		PLURAL	
	m	f	m	f
this, these	este	esta	estos	estas
that, those	ese	esa	esos	esas
that, those (over there)	aquel	aquella	aquellos	aquellas

All of these words are also used as demonstrative pronouns ('this one', 'that one', etc.). In this case they're written with an accent: éste, ésos, aquél, etc.

There are also 'neuter' forms: esto, eso, aquello. They are used when no specific noun is being referred to, e.g.:

esto es imposible (this is impossible).

✳ subject pronouns (I, you, he, she, etc.)

I	yo
you (informal)*	tú
you (formal)*	usted
he	él
she	ella
we	nosotros (masculine), nosotras (feminine)
you (informal)*	vosotros (masculine), vosotras (feminine)
you (formal)*	ustedes
they	ellos (masculine), ellas (feminine)

(*see 'You' below)

These pronouns are not used much – Spanish verbs have different endings which show what the subject is (see Verbs below). Usted and ustedes tend to be used more than the others, to show politeness, but in general the subject pronouns are used mainly for emphasis or to avoid confusion, e.g.: él es inglés, ella es escocesa (he is English, she is Scottish).

✳ you

In English there is only one way of addressing people using the word 'you'. In Spanish, there are two ways – one is more polite/formal, the other more casual/informal.

The informal way is used between friends and relatives, between people of the same age group, and to children. The part of the verb used is the second person (singular or plural as appropriate). The word for 'you' is tú (vosotros/vosotras in the plural).

The formal way uses the third person of the verb (singular or plural). The word for 'you' is usted (ustedes in the plural). Most of the phrases in this book use the formal way of saying 'you'.

✳ object pronouns

These are the equivalent of 'me', 'him', 'it', 'us', etc. Spanish has both direct object and indirect object pronouns. (Indirect objects are the equivalent of 'to/for me', 'to/for us', etc.)

The same words are used for both types, except in the third person. The full list is:

PERSON	SINGULAR	PLURAL
first	me	nos
second	te	os
third		
– direct	lo, la	los, las
– indirect	le	les

They generally come before the verb, e.g.:

lo hablo bien (I speak it well)

¿le está esperando? (is he/she expecting you?)

But they can be added to the end of an infinitive of a verb, e.g.: ¿puede decirle que me llame? (can you tell him/her to call me?).

✳ verbs

Spanish verbs have different endings according to (i) the subject of the verb, (ii) the tense. There are three main groups of verbs, with different sets of endings for each group.

In dictionaries, verbs are listed in the infinitive form which ends in -ar, -er or -ir (these are the three groups). Below are the endings for the present tense of these three groups:

	-AR	-ER	-IR
	hablar	**comer**	**vivir**
yo	hablo	como	vivo
tú	hablas	comes	vives
él, ella, usted	habla	come	vive
nosotros/as	hablamos	comemos	vivimos
vosotros/as	habláis	coméis	vivís
ellos/as, ustedes	hablan	comen	viven

✳ to be

There are two Spanish verbs meaning 'to be': ser and estar. Estar is used for temporary states and for locations, e.g.:
estoy de vacaciones (I am on holiday)
está enfermo (he is ill)
el banco está allá (the bank is over there).

Otherwise ser is used, e.g.: soy inglés (I am English)
España es un país bonito (Spain is a beautiful country)

Ser and estar are both irregular:

	SER	ESTAR
yo	soy	estoy
tú	eres	estás
él, ella, usted	es	está
nosotros/as	somos	estamos
vosotros/as	sois	estáis
ellos/as, ustedes	son	están

✻ other irregular verbs

Other common verbs that are also irregular include:

TENER	IR	PODER	QUERER	VENIR
(to have)	(to go)	(to be able)	(to want; to love)	(to come)
tengo	voy	puedo	quiero	vengo
tienes	vas	puedes	quieres	vienes
tiene	va	puede	quiere	viene
tenemos	vamos	podemos	queremos	venimos
tenéis	vais	podéis	queréis	venís
tienen	van	pueden	quieren	vienen

Parts of other irregular verbs are given in the Dictionary.

✻ other verb tenses

A few verbs in other tenses that you may find useful:

ir (to go)	I went	fui
	we went	fuimos
	I used to go	iba
	we used to go	íbamos
ser (to be)	I was/used to be	era
	we were/used to be	éramos
estar (to be)	I was	estuve
	we were	estuvimos
	I have been	he estado
	we have been	hemos estado
tener (to have)	I had/used to have	tenía
	we had/used to have	teníamos
venir (to come)	I came	vine
	we came	vinimos
	I used to come	venía
	we used to come	veníamos

basic grammar

For talking about the future, you can often use the present tense, e.g.: mañana juego al tenis (tomorrow I am playing tennis)

In a similar way to English, you can also say 'I am going to...', using the verb ir, followed by a and an infinitive, e.g.:
mañana voy a jugar al tenis (tomorrow I am going to play tennis)
vamos a ir a Granada (we are going to go to Granada)

❋ negatives

To make a verb negative, put no before it, e.g.:
no tengo hijos (I don't have any children)
no entiendo (I don't understand)
el señor García no está (Mr García isn't in)

Spanish has double negatives, e.g.:
no tengo nada (I don't have anything) (nada literally means 'nothing').

❋ questions

When a question does not begin with a question word ('where?', 'how?', 'why?', etc.), the word order is generally the same as it would be in an ordinary statement. The intonation of the voice changes to make it a question, e.g.:
hay un bar en la plaza (there is a bar in the square)
¿hay un bar en la plaza? (is there a bar in the square?)

Note that, in writing, questions begin with an upside-down question mark. The same happens with exclamations:
¡Viva España!

English – Spanish dictionary

There's a list of **car parts** on page 59 and **parts of the body** on page 143. See also the **menu reader** on page 91, and **numbers** on page 14.

Spanish nouns are given with their gender in brackets: (m) for masculine and (f) for feminine, (m/f) for those which can be either, (pl) = plural.

Adjectives which have different endings for masculine and feminine are shown like this: blanco/a (i.e. blanco for masculine, blanca for feminine). See **basic grammar**, page 152, for further explanation.

A

a, an un/una/unos/unas *oon/oona/oonos/oonas*

abbey abadía (f) *abadeea*

about *(relating to)* sobre *sobre (approximately)* unos/unas *oonos/oonas*

above sobre *sobre*

abroad en el extranjero *en el extranhhero*

abscess absceso (m) *abstheso*

to **accept** *(take)* aceptar *atheptar*

accident accidente (m) *aktheedente*

accommodation alojamiento (m) *alohhamyento*

account *(bank)* cuenta (f) *kwenta*

ache dolor (m) *dolor*

acid ácido/a *atheedo/a*

across a través *a trabes (opposite)* enfrente *enfrente*

actor actor (m)/actriz (f) *aktor/aktreeth*

adaptor adaptador (m) *adaptador*

address dirección (f) *deerekthyon*

admission admisión (f) *admeesyon*

admission charge precio (m) de entrada (f) *prethyo de entrada*

adopted adoptado/a *adoptado/a*

adult adulto/a *adoolto/a*

advance *(early payment)* anticipo (m) *anteetheepo*

» **in advance** por adelantado *por adelantado*

advanced *(level)* avanzado/a *abanthado/a*

advertisement anuncio (m) *anoonthyo*

advertising publicidad (f) *poobleetheedad*

aerial antena (f) *antena*

aeroplane avión (m) *abyon*

afford: I can't afford it no me lo puedo permitir *no me lo pwedo permeeteer*

afraid: I'm afraid me temo *me temo*

after después de *despwes de*

afterwards después *despwes*

afternoon tarde (f) *tarde*

aftershave aftershave (m) *aftersheif*

again de nuevo *de nwebo*

against contra *kontra*

age edad (f) *edad*

agency agencia (f) *ahhenthya*

ago hace *athe*

to **agree** estar de acuerdo *estar de akwerdo*

AIDS SIDA (m) *seeda*

air aire (m) *iyre*

» **(by) air mail** (por) correo aéreo *(por) korreo aereo*

air conditioning aire acondicionado (m) *iyre akondeethyonado*

air force ejército del aire (m) *ehhertheeto del iyre*

airline línea aérea (f) *leenea aerea*

airport aeropuerto (m) *aeropwerto*

aisle pasillo (m) *paseelyo*

alarm alarma (f) *alarma*

alarm clock despertador (m) *despertador*

alcohol alcohol (m) *alkol*

alcoholic *(content)* alcohólico/a *alkooleeko/a* (person) alcohólico/a *alkooleeko/a*

alive vivo/a *beebo/a*

all todo *todo*

allergic to alérgico a a *alerhheeko/a a*

alley callejón *calyehhon*

to allow permitir *permeeteer*

allowed permitido/a *permeeteedo/a*

all right *(OK)* vale *bale*

alone solo/a *solo/a*

along a lo largo de *a lo largo de*

already ya *ya*

also también *tambyen*

although aunque *ownke*

always siempre *syempre*

ambassador embajador (m) *embahhador*

ambition ambición (f) *ambeethyon*

ambulance ambulancia (f) *amboolanthya*

among entre *entre*

amount *(money)* cantidad (f) *kanteedad*

amusement park parque de atracciones (m) *parke de atrakthyones*

anaesthetic *(local)* anestesia (f) (local) *anestesya (lokal) (general)* general hheneral

and y *ee*

angry enfadado/a *enfadado/a*

ankle tobillo (m) *tobeelyo*

animal animal (m) *aneemal*

anniversary aniversario (m) *aneebersaryo*

annoyed enfadado/a *enfadado/a*

another otro/a *otro/a*

answer respuesta (f) *respwesta*

to answer responder *responder*

antibiotic antibiótico (m) *anteebyoteeko*

antifreeze anticongelante (m) *anteekonhhelante*

antique *(noun)* antigüedad (f) *anteegwedad*

antique *(adj.)* antiguo/a *anteegwo/a*

antiseptic antiséptico/a *anteesepteeko/a*

anxious ansioso/a *ansyoso/a*

any algún/alguna, algo *algoon/algoona, algo*

anyone alguien *algyen*

anything algo *algo*

anything else algo más *algo mas*

anyway de todos modos *de todos modos*

anywhere cualquier sitio/parte *kwalkyer seeteeo/parte*

apart (from) aparte (de) *aparte (de)*

apartment apartamento (m) *apartamento*

appendicitis apendicitis (f) *apendeetheetees*

apple manzana (f) *manthana*

appointment cita (f) *theeta*

approximately aproximadamente *aproxeemadamente*

arch arco (m) *arko*

archaeology arqueología (f) *arkeolohheea*

architect arquitecto/a *arkeetekto/a*

area área (m) *area*

argument discusión (f) *deeskoosyon*

arm brazo (m) *bratho*

armbands *(swimming)* flotador *flotador*

army ejército (m) *ehhertheeto*

around alrededor (de) *alrededor de*

to arrange *(fix)* arreglar *arreglar*

arrest: under arrest detenido/a *deteneedo/a*

arrival llegada (f) *lyegada*

to arrive llegar *lyegar*
art arte (m) *arte*
» fine arts bellas artes (f/pl) *belyas artes*
art gallery galería de arte (f) *galereea de arte*
arthritis artritis (f) *artreetees*
article artículo (m) *arteekoolo*
artificial artificial *arteefeethyal*
artist artista (m/f) *arteesta*
as *(like)* como *komo*
ash ceniza (f) *theneetha*
ashtray cenicero (m) *theneethero*
to ask preguntar *pregoontar*
aspirin aspirina (f) *aspeereena*
assistant ayudante (m/f) *ayoodante*
asthma asma (m) *asma*
at a, en a, *en*
» *(@)* arroba *arroba*
athletics atletismo (m) *atleteesmo*
atmosphere atmósfera (f) *atmosfera*
to attack atacar *atakar*
» *(mug)* asaltar *asaltar*
attendant *(bathing)* encargado/a *enkargado/a*
attractive atractivo/a *atrakteebo/a*
aunt tía (f) *teea*
automatic automático/a *owtomateeko/a*
autumn otoño *otonyo*
avalanche avalancha *abalancha*
to avoid evitar *ebeetar*
away (from) lejos (de) *lehhos (de)*
awful espantoso/a *espantoso/a*

B

baby bebé (m) *bebe*
baby food comida para bebés (f) *komeeda para bebes*
baby wipes toallitas limpiadoras (f/pl) *toalyeetas leempyadoras*
baby's bottle biberón (m) *beeberon*
babysitter canguro (m/f) *kangooro*
back *(reverse side)* dorso (m) *dorso*
» at the back atrás *atras*
backwards hacia atrás *athya atras*

bacon beicon (m) *baykon*
bad malo/a *malo/a*
bag bolsa (f) *bolsa*
baggage equipaje (m) *ekeepahhe*
baker's panadería (f) *panadereea*
balcony balcón (m) *balkon (theatre)* anfiteatro (m) *anfeeteatro*
bald calvo/a *kalbo/a*
ball *(tennis, etc.)* pelota (f) *pelota* *(football)* balón (m) *balon*
ballet ballet (m) *balet*
banana plátano (m) *platano*
band *(music)* banda (f) *banda*
bandage venda (f) *benda*
bank *(money)* banco (m) *banko*
banker banquero (m) *bankero*
bar bar (m) *bar*
barber's peluquería (f) *pelookereea*
bargain oferta (f) *oferta*
baseball cap gorra (f) *gorra*
basement sótano (m) *sotano*
basin *(sink)* lavabo (m) *lababo*
basket cesta (f) *thesta*
basketball baloncesto (m) *balonthesto*
bath baño (m) *banyo*
» to have a bath tomar un baño *tomar oon banyo*
to bathe bañarse *banyarse*
bathing costume traje de baño (m) *trahhe de banyo*
bathroom baño (m) *banyo*
battery pila (f) *peela (car)* batería (f) *batereea*
bay bahía (f) *baeea*
to be ser/estar *ser/estar*
beach playa (f) *playa*
beans judías (f/pl) *hhoodyas*
beard barba (f) *barba*
beautiful bonito/a *boneeto/a*
because porque *porke*
bed cama (f) *kama*
bedroom habitación (f) *abeetathyon*
bee abeja (f) *abehha*
beef carne de vaca (f) *karne de baka*

beer cerveza (f) *therbetha*

before antes (de) *antes (de)*

to **begin** empezar *empethar*

beginner principiante (m/f) *preentheepyante*

beginning principio (m) *preentheepyo*

behind detrás (de) *detras de*

beige beige *beis*

to **believe** creer *kreer*

  » **I believe so/not** creo que sí/no *kreo ke see/no*

bell campana (f) *kampana (doorbell)* timbre (m) *teembre*

to **belong to** pertenecer a *pertenether a*

below abajo *abahho*

belt cinturón (m) *theentooron*

bend curva (f) *koorba*

berry baya (f) *baya*

berth litera (f) *leetera (on ship)* camarote (f) *kamarote*

besides además *ademas*

best (el/la/lo) mejor *(el/la/lo) mehhor*

better mejor *mehhor*

between entre *entre*

beyond más allá (de) *mas alya (de)*

bib babero (m) *babero*

Bible Biblia (f) *beebleea*

bicycle bicicleta *beetheecleta*

big grande *grande*

bigger más grande *mas grande*

bill cuenta (f) *kwenta*

bin (rubbish) cubo de la basura (m) *koobo de la basoora*

bin liners bolsas para la basura (f/pl) *bolsas para la basoora*

binding (ski) fijación (f) *feehhathyon*

binoculars prismáticos (m/pl) *preesmateekos*

biology biología *byolohheea*

bird pájaro (m) *pahharo*

birthday cumpleaños (m) *koompleanyos*

biscuit galleta (f) *galyeta*

bit un poco *oon poko*

to **bite** morder *morder*

bitter amargo/a *amargo/a*

black negro/a *negro/a*

  » **black coffee** café solo *kafe solo*

blackcurrant grosella (f) *groselya*

blanket manta (f) *manta*

beach playa (f) *playa*

to **bleed** sangrar *sangrar*

blind ciego/a *thyego/a*

blister ampolla (f) *ampolya*

to **block** (road) obstruir, cerrar *obstrweer, therrar*

blocked obstruido/a *obstrweedo/a* (road) cerrado/a *therrado/a*

blonde rubio/a *roobyo/a*

blood sangre (f) *sangre*

blouse blusa (f) *blooosa*

to **blow** soplar *soplar*

to **blow-dry** secar a mano (m) *sekar a mano*

blue azul *athool*

to **board** embarcar *embarkar*

boarding card tarjeta de embarque (f) *tarhheta de embarke*

boat barco (m) *barko*

boat trip viaje en barco (m) *byahhe en barko*

body cuerpo (m) *kwerpo*

to **boil** hervir *erbeer*

  » **boiled egg** huevo pasado por agua (m) *webo pasado por agwa*

boiler calentador (m) *kalentador*

bomb bomba (f) *bomba*

bone hueso (m) *weso*

book libro (m) *leebro*

to **book** reservar *reserbar*

booking reserva (f) *reserba*

booking office (rail) despacho de billetes (m) *despacho de beelyetes*

bookshop librería (f) *leebrereea*

boot (shoe) bota (f) *bota*

border (edge) borde (m) *borde* (frontier) frontera (f) *frontera*

boring aburrido/a *aboorreedo/a*

both ambos/as *ambos/as*

bottle botella (f) *botelya*

bottle opener abrebotellas (m) *abrebotelyas*

bottom fondo (m) *fondo*

bow *(ship)* proa (f) *proa*

bowl tazón (m) *tathon*

box caja (f) *kahha* (theatre) palco (m) *palko*

box office taquilla (f) *takeelya*

boy chico (m) *cheeko*

boyfriend novio (m) *nobyo*

bra sostén (m) *sosten*

bracelet pulsera (f) *poolsera*

brain cerebro (m) *therebro*

branch rama (f) *rama* (bank etc.) sucursal (f) *sookoorsal*

brand marca (f) *marka*

brandy coñac (m) *konyak*

brass latón (m) *laton*

brave valiente *balyente*

bread pan (m) *pan*

bread roll bollo (m) *bolyo*

to break *(inc. limb)* romper *romper*

breakdown truck grúa (f) *grooa*

breakfast desayuno (m) *desayoono*

breast pecho (m) *pecho* (of chicken) pechuga (f) *pechooga*

to breathe respirar *respeerar*

bridge puente (m) *pwente*

briefcase maletín (m) *maleteen*

bright *(colour)* vivo/a *beebo/a* (light) brillante *breelyante*

to bring traer *traer*

British británico *breetaneeko*

broad ancho/a *ancho/a*

brochure folleto (m) *folyeto*

broken roto/a *roto/a*

bronchitis bronquitis (f) *bronkeetees*

bronze bronce (m) *bronthe*

brooch broche (m) *broche*

broom escoba (f) *eskoba*

brother hermano (m) *ermano*

brother-in-law cuñado (m) *koonyado*

brown marrón *marron*

bruise cardenal (m) *kardenal*

brush cepillo (m) *thepeelyo*

bucket cubo (m) *koobo*

buffet buffet (m) *boofe*

to build construir *konstrweer*

builder albañil (m) *albanyeel*

building edificio (m) *edeefeethyo*

building site obra (f) *obra*

bulb *(light)* bombilla (f) *bombeelya*

bull toro (m) *toro*

burn *(on skin)* quemadura (f) *kemadoora*

burnt *(food)* quemado/a *kemado/a*

bus autobús (m) *owtoboos*
   » **by bus** en autobús *en owtoboos*

bus-driver conductor de autobuses (m) *kondooktor de owtobooses*

bush arbusto (m) *arboosto*

business negocios (m/pl) *negothyos*
   » **on business** de negocios *de negothyos*

bus station estación de autobuses (f) *estathyon de owtobooses*

bus stop parada de autobús (f) *parada de owtoboos*

busy ocupado/a *okoopado/a*

but pero *pero*

butane gas gas butano (m) *gas bootano*

butcher's carnicería (f) *karneethereea*

butter mantequilla (f) *mantekeelya*

butterfly mariposa (f) *mareeposa*

button botón (m) *boton*

to buy comprar *komprar*

by *(author etc.)* por *por*

C

cabin camarote (m) *kamarote*

cable car teleférico (m) *telefereeko*

café cafetería (f) *kafetereea*

cake pastel (m) *pastel*

cake shop pastelería (f) *pastelereea*

calculator calculadora (f) *kalkooladora*

call *(phone)* llamada (f) *lyamada*

to call llamar *lyamar*

» **to be called** llamarse *lyamarse*

calm tranquilo/a *trankeelo/a*

camera cámara (f) *kamara*

to **camp** acampar *akampar*

camp bed cama plegable (f) *kama plegable*

camping camping (m) *kampeen*

campsite camping (m) *kampeen*

can *(to be able)* poder *poder*

can *(tin)* lata (f) *lata*

can opener abrelatas (m) *abrelatas*

to **cancel** cancelar *kanthelar*

cancer cáncer (m) *kanther*

candle vela (f) *bela*

canoe canoa (f) *kanoa*

capital *(city)* capital (f) *kapeetal*

captain *(boat)* capitán (m) *kapeetan*

car coche (m) *koche*

» **by car** en coche *en koche*

car hire alquiler de coches (m) *alkeeler de koches*

car park aparcamiento (m) *aparkamyento*

carafe garrafa (f) *garrafa*

caravan caravana (f) *karabana*

caravan site camping (m) *kampeen*

cardigan rebeca (f) *rebeka*

care: I don't care no me importa *no me eemporta*

care: to take care tener cuidado *tener kweedado*

career carrera (f) *karrera*

careful cuidadoso/a *kweedadoso/a*

careless descuidado/a *deskweedado/a*

carpet alfombra (f) *alfombra*

carriage *(rail)* vagón (m) *bagon*

carrier bag bolsa (f) *bolsa*

to **carry** llevar *lyebar*

to **carry on** *(walking/driving)* continuar *konteenwar*

car wash lavado automático (m) *labado owtomateeko*

case: in case por si acaso *por see akaso*

cash dinero en efectivo (m) *deenero en efekteebo*

» **to pay cash** pagar al contado *pagar al kontado*

to **cash** cobrar *kobrar*

cash desk, cashier caja (f) *kahha*

cassette cinta, cassette (f) *theenta, kaset*

castle *(palace)* castillo (m) *kasteelyo*

» *(fortress)* fortaleza (f) *fortaletha*

cat gato/a *gato/a*

catalogue catálogo (m) *katalogo*

to **catch** *(train/bus)* coger *kohher*

cathedral catedral (f) *katedral*

Catholic católico/a *katoleeko/a*

to **cause** causar *kowsar*

caution precaución (f) *prekowthyon*

cave cueva (f) *kweba*

CD CD (m) *thede*

CD-Rom CD-Rom (m) *thede rom*

ceiling techo (m) *techo*

cellar sótano (m) *sotano* *(wine)* bodega (f) *bodega*

cemetery cementerio (m) *thementeryo*

centimetre centímetro (m) *thenteemetro*

central central *thentral*

central heating calefacción central (f) *kalefakthyon thentral*

centre centro (m) *thentro*

century siglo (m) *seeglo*

certain seguro/a *segooro/a*

certainly ¿cómo no? *komo no*

certificate certificado (m) *therteefeekado*

chain cadena (f) *kadena*

chair silla (f) *seelya*

chair lift telesilla (f) *teleseelya*

chalet chalet (m) *chale*

champagne champán (m) *champan*

change *(small coins)* suelto (m) *swelto*

to **change** *(clothes)* cambiarse *kambyarse* *(money, trains, etc.)* cambiar *kambyar*

changing room probador (m) *probador*

chapel capilla (f) *kapeelya*

charcoal carbón (m) *karbon*

charge *(money)* precio (m) *prethyo*

charger *(phone)* cargador (m) *kargador*

charter flight vuelo chárter (m) *bwelo charter*

cheap barato/a *barato/a*

to check comprobar *komprobar*

check-in *(desk)* mostrador de facturación (m) *mostrador de faktoorathyon*

to check in facturar *faktoorar*

cheek mejilla (f) *mehheelya*

cheeky descarado/a *deskarado/a*

cheers! ¡salud! *salood*

cheese queso *keso*

chef jefe/a de cocina *hhefe/a de kotheena*

chemist's farmacia (f) *farmathya*

cheque cheque (m) *cheke*

chess ajedrez (m) *ahhedreth*

chewing gum chicle (m) *cheecle*

chicken pollo (m) *polyo*

chickenpox varicela (f) *bareethela*

child niño/a *neenyo/a*

children *(sons and daughters)* hijos/as *eehhos/as*

chimney chimenea (f) *cheemenea*

chin barbilla (f) *barbeelya*

china porcelana (f) *porthelana*

chips patatas fritas (f/pl) *patatas freetas*

chocolate chocolate (m) *chokolate*

to choose elegir *elehheer*

Christian cristiano/a *kreestyano/a*

Christian name nombre de pila (m) *nombre de peela*

Christmas Navidad (f) *nabeedad*

Christmas Day Día de Navidad (m) *deea de nabeedad*

Christmas Eve Nochebuena (f) *nochebwena*

church iglesia (f) *eeglesya*

cigar puro (m) *pooro*

cigarette cigarrillo (m) *theegarreelyo*

cigarette paper papel de liar (m) *papel de lyar*

cinema cine (m) *theene*

circle círculo (m) *theerkoolo (theatre)* anfiteatro (m) *anfeeteatro*

city ciudad (f) *thyoodad*

civil servant funcionario/a *foonthyonaryo/a*

class clase (f) *klase*

classical music música clásica (f) *mooseeka klasika*

claustrophobia claustrofobia (f) *klowstrofobya*

to clean limpiar *leempyar*

clean limpio/a *leempyo/a*

cleaner limpiador/a *leempyador/a*

cleansing lotion loción limpiadora (f) *lothyon leempyadora*

clear claro/a *klaro/a*

clerk oficinista (m/f) *ofeetheeneesta*

clever inteligente *eenteleehhente*

to click *(computer)* hacer clic *ather klik*

cliff acantilado (m) *akanteelado*

climate clima (m) *kleema*

to climb subir *soobeer*

climber alpinista (m/f) *alpeeneesta*

clinic clínica *kleeneeka*

cloakroom guardarropa (m) *gwardarropa*

clock reloj (m) *reloj*

close *(by)* cerca *therka*

to close cerrar *therrar*

closed cerrado/a *therrado/a*

cloth trapo (m) *trapo*

clothes ropa (f) *ropa*

clothes pegs pinzas (f/pl) *peenthas*

cloud nube (f) *noobe*

cloudy nuboso *nooboso*

club club (m) *kloob*

coach autocar (m) *owtokar (railway)* vagón (m) *bagon*

coast costa (f) *kosta*

coat abrigo (m) *abreego*

coat-hanger percha (f) *percha*

cocktail cóctel (m) *koktel*

coffee café (m) *kafe*

coin moneda (f) *moneda*

cold frío/a *freeo/a*

» **to have a cold** tener un resfriado *tener oon resfryado*

collar cuello (m) *kwelyo*

colleague colega (m/f) *kolega*

to **collect** coleccionar *kolekthyonar*

collection (postal/rubbish) recogida (f) *rekohheeda*

college colegio (m) *kolehhyo*

colour color (m) *kolor*

colour-blind daltoniano/a *daltonyano/a*

comb peine (m) *payne*

to **come** venir *beneer*

to **come back** volver *bolber*

to **come in** entrar *entrar*

comedy comedia (f) *comedya*

comfortable cómodo/a *komodo/a*

comic (magazine) tebeo (m) *tebeo*

commercial comercial *komerthyal*

common (usual) común *komoon* (shared) compartido/a *komparteedo/a*

communism comunismo (m) *komooneesmo*

company compañía (f) *kompanyeea*

compared with comparado/a con *komparado/a kon*

compartment compartimento (m) *komparteemento*

compass brújula (f) *broohhoola*

to **complain** reclamar *reklamar*

complaint reclamación (f) *reklamathyon*

complete (finished) completo/a *kompleto/a (whole)* entero/a *entero/a*

complicated complicado/a *kompleekado/a*

compulsory obligatorio/a *obleegatoryo/a*

composer compositor (m) *komposeetor*

computer ordenador (m) *ordenador*

concert concierto (m) *konthyerto*

concert hall sala de conciertos (f) *sala de konthyertos*

concussion concusión (f) *konkoosyon*

condition (state) condición (f) *kondeethyon*

conditioner acondicionador (m) *akondeethyonador*

condom condón (m) *kondon*

conference conferencia (f) *konferenthya*

to **confirm** confirmar *konfeermar*

conjunctivitis conjuntivitis (f) *konhhoonteebeetees*

connection conexión (f) *konexyon*

conscious consciente *konsthyente*

conservation conservación (f) *konserbathyon*

conservative conservador/a *konserbador/a*

constipation estreñimiento (m) *estrenyeemyento*

consulate consulado (m) *konsoolado*

consultant (medicine) especialista (m/f) *espethyaleesta*

contact lenses lentillas (f/pl) *lenteelyas*

continent continente (m) *konteenente*

contraceptive anticonceptivo (m) *anteekonthepteebo*

contract contrato (m) *kontrato*

control (passport) control (m) *kontrol*

convent convento (m) *konbento*

convenient conveniente *konbenyente*

cook cocinero/a *kotheenero/a*

to **cook** cocinar *kotheenar*

cooked cocido/a *kotheedo/a*

cooker cocina (f) *kotheena*

cool fresco/a *fresko/a*

cool box nevera portátil (f) *nebera portateel*

copper cobre (m) *kobre*

copy copia (f) *kopya (book)* ejemplar (m) *ehhemplar*

corkscrew sacacorchos (m) *sakakorchos*

corner (outside) esquina (f) *eskeena (room)* rincón (m) *reenkon*

correct correcto/a *korrekto/a*

corridor pasillo (m) *paseelyo*
cosmetics cosméticos (m/pl) *kosmeteekos*
to **cost** costar *kostar*
cot cuna (f) *koona*
cottage casita de campo (f) *kaseeta de kampo*
cotton *(material)* algodón (m) *algodon* *(thread)* hilo (m) *eelo*
cotton wool algodón (m) *algodon*
couchette litera (f) *leetera*
cough tos (f) *tos*
to **cough** toser *toser*
to **count** contar *kontar*
counter *(post office)* mostrador (m) *mostrador*
country país (m) *paees*
country(side) campo (m) *kampo*
couple *(pair)* pareja (f) *parehha*
course *(lessons)* curso (m) *koorso*
court *(law)* tribunal (m) *treeboonal* *(tennis)* pista (f) *peesta*
cousin primo/a *preemo/a*
cover *(lid)* cubierta (f) *koobyerta*
cow vaca (f) *baka*
crab cangrejo (m) *kangrehho*
cramp calambre (m) *kalambre*
crazy loco/a *loko/a*
cream nata (f) *nata (lotion)* crema (f) *krema (colour)* crema *krema*
credit card tarjeta de crédito (f) *tarhheta de kredeeto*
crisps patatas fritas (f/pl) *patatas freetas*
cross cruz (f) *krooth*
to **cross** *(border)* cruzar *kroothar*
cross-country skiing esquí de fondo (m) *eskee de fondo*
crossing *(sea)* travesía (f) *traveseea*
crossroads cruce (m) *kroothe*
crowd multitud (f) *moolteetood*
crowded abarrotado/a *abarrotado/a*
crown corona (f) *korona*
cruise crucero (m) *kroothero*
crutch muleta (f) *mooleta*

to **cry** llorar *lyorar*
crystal cristal (m) *kreestal*
cup taza (f) *tatha*
cupboard armario (m) *armaryo*
cure *(remedy)* remedio (m) *remedyo*
to **cure** curar *koorar*
curler *(hair)* rulo (m) *roolo*
curly rizado/a *reethado/a*
current *(electrical)* corriente (f) *korryente*
curtain cortina (f) *korteena*
curve curva (f) *koorba*
cushion cojín (m) *kohheen*
customs aduana (f) *adwana*
cut corte (m) *korte*
to **cut** cortar *kortar*
to **cut oneself** cortarse *kortarse*
cutlery cubiertos (m) *koobyertos*
cycling ciclismo (m) *theekleesmo*
cyclist ciclista (m) *theekleesta*
cystitis cistitis (f) *theesteetees*

D

daily diario/a *dyaryo/a*
damage daño (m) *danyo*
to **damage** dañar *danyar*
damp húmedo/a *oomedo/a*
dance baile (m) *biyle*
to **dance** bailar *biylar*
danger peligro (m) *peleegro*
dangerous peligroso/a *peleegroso/a*
dark oscuro/a *oskooro/a*
data datos (m/pl) *datos*
date *(day)* fecha (f) *fecha*
daughter hija (f) *eehha*
daughter-in-law nuera (f) *nwera*
day día (m) *deea*
day after tomorrow pasado mañana *pasado manyana*
day before yesterday anteayer *anteayer*
dead muerto/a *mwerto/a*
deaf sordo/a *sordo/a*
dear *(loved)* querido/a *kereedo/a* *(expensive)* caro/a *karo/a*

D

dictionary

death muerte (f) *mwerte*
debt deuda (f) *deooda*
decaffeinated descafeinado/a *deskafaynado/a*
deck cubierta (f) *koobyerta*
deckchair tumbona (f) *toombona*
to decide decidir *detheedeer*
to declare declarar *deklarar*
deep profundo/a *profoondo/a*
deer ciervo (m) *thyerbo*
defect defecto (m) *defekto*
definitely definitivamente *defeeneeteebamente*
to defrost descongelar *deskonhhelar*
degree *(temperature)* grado (m) *grado* (university) título (m) *teetoolo*
delay retraso (m) *retraso*
delicate delicado/a *deleekado/a*
delicious delicioso/a *deleethyoso/a*
to deliver entregar *entregar*
delivery entrega (f) *entrega*
demonstration manifestación (f) *maneefestathyon*
denim tela vaquera (f) *tela bakera*
dentist dentista (m/f) *denteesta*
denture dentadura postiza (f) *dentadoora posteetha*
deodorant desodorante (m) *desodorante*
to depart *(transport)* salir *saleer*
department departamento (m) *departamento*
department store grandes almacenes (m) *grandes almathenes*
departure *(transport)* salida (f) *saleeda*
departure lounge sala de embarque (f) *sala de embarke*
deposit depósito (m) *deposeeto*
desert desierto (m) *desyerto*
to describe describir *deskreebeer*
description descripción (f) *deskreepthyon*
design diseño (m) *deesenyo*
to design diseñar *deesenyar*
designer diseñador/a *deesenyador/a*
dessert postre (m) *postre*

destination destino (m) *desteeno*
detail detalle (m) *detalye*
detergent detergente (m) *deterhhente*
to develop *(film)* revelar *rebelar*
diabetes diabetes (f) *dyabetes*
diabetic diabético/a *dyabeteeko/a*
to dial marcar *markar*
dialling code prefijo (m) *prefeehho*
dialling tone tono de marcar (m) *tono de markar*
diamond diamante (m) *dyamante*
diarrhoea diarrea (f) *dyarrea*
diary agenda (f) *ahhenda*
dice dado (m) *dado*
dictionary diccionario (m) *dikthyonaryo*
to die morir *moreer*
diesel gasóleo, gas-oil (m) *gasoleo, gas-oeel*
diet dieta (f) *dyeta*
different distinto/a *deesteento/a*
difficult difícil *deefeetheel*
digital digital *deehheetal*
digital camera cámara digital *kamara deehheetal*
dining room comedor (m) *komedor*
dinner cena (f) *thena*
direct *(train)* directo/a *deerekto/a*
direction dirección (f) *deerekthyon*
director director/a *deerektor/a*
directory *(telephone)* guía telefónica (f) *geea telefoneeka*
dirty sucio/a *soothyo/a*
disabled minusválido/a *meenoosbaleedo/a*
disappointed decepcionado/a *dethepthyonado/a*
disc disco (m) *deesko*
disco discoteca (f) *deeskoteka*
discount descuento (m) *deskwento*
dish plato (m) *plato*
dishwasher lavavajillas (f) *lababahheelyas*
disinfectant desinfectante (m) *deseenfektante*

170

dislocated dislocado/a *deeslokado/a*

disposable desechable *desechable*

disposable nappies dodotis (m) *dodotees*

distance distancia (f) *deestanthya*

distilled water (el) agua destilada (f) *agwa desteelada*

district zona (f), barrio (m) *thona, barryo*

to dive tirarse al agua *teerarse al agwa*

diversion desviación (f) *desbyathyon*

diving submarinismo (m) *soobmareeneesmo*

divorced divorciado/a *deeborthyado/a*

dizzy mareado/a *mareado/a*

DJ pinchadiscos (m/f) *peenchadeeskos*

to do hacer *ather*

doctor médico (m) *medeeko*

document documento (m) *dokoomento*

dog perro (m) *perro*

doll muñeca (f) *moonyeka*

dollar dólar (m) *dolar*

dome cúpula (f) *koopoola*

donkey burro (m) *boorro*

door puerta (f) *pwerta*

dot com punto com *poonto kom*

double doble *doble*

double bed cama matrimonial (f) *kama matreemonyal*

down (movement) abajo *abahho*

to download descargar *deskargar*

downstairs abajo *abahho*

drain (in the street) alcantarilla (f) *alkantareelya*

drama drama (m) *drama*

draught (air) corriente (f) *korryente*

draught beer cerveza de barril (f) *therbetha de barreel*

to draw dibujar *deeboohhar*

drawer cajón (m) *kahhon*

drawing dibujo (m) *deeboohho*

dreadful espantoso/a *espantoso/a*

dress vestido (m) *besteedo*

to dress, get dressed vestir, vestirse *besteer, besteerse*

dressing (medical) vendaje (m) *bendahhe* (salad) aliño (m) *aleenyo*

drink bebida (f) *bebeeda*

to drink beber *beber*

to drip gotear *gotear*

to drive conducir *kondootheer*

driver conductor *kondooktor*

driving licence carné de conducir (m) *karne de kondootheer*

to drown ahogar *aogar*

drug (medication) medicamento (m) *medeekamento* (illicit) droga (f) *droga*

drug addict drogadicto/a *drogadeekto/a*

drum tambor (m) *tambor*

drunk borracho/a *borracho/a*

dry seco/a *seko/a*

dry-cleaner's tintorería (f) *teentorereea*

duck pato (m) *pato*

dull (weather) gris *grees*

dumb mudo/a *moodo/a*

dummy (baby's) chupete (m) *choopete*

during durante *doorante*

dust polvo (m) *polbo*

dustbin cubo de la basura (m) *koobo de la basoora*

duty (tax) impuesto (m) *eempwesto*

duty-free libre de impuestos *leebre de eempwestos*

duvet edredón (m) *edredon*

DVD DVD (m) *de oobe de*

dyslexic disléxico/a *deeslexeeko/a*

E

each cada *kada*

ear oído (m) *oeedo* (outer ear) oreja (f) *orehha*

earache dolor de oídos (m) *dolor de oeedos*

eardrops gotas para los oídos (f) *gotas para los oeedos*

earlier antes *antes*

early temprano *temprano*

to earn ganar *ganar*

earring pendiente (m) *pendyente*

earth tierra (f) *tyerra*

earthquake terremoto (m) *terremoto*

east este (m) *este*

eastern del este, oriental *del este, oryental*

Easter Semana Santa (f) *semana santa*

easy fácil *fatheel*

to **eat** comer *komer*

economical económico/a *ekonomeeko/a*

economics economía (f) *ekonomeea*

economy economía (f) *ekonomeea*

edible comestible *komesteeble*

either cualquiera *kwalkyera*

either... or... o ... o... *o ... o...*

elastic band goma elástica (f) **go**ma *elasteeka*

election elección (f) *elekthyon*

electric eléctrico/a *elektreeko/a*

electrician electricista (m/f) *elektreetheesta*

electricity electricidad (f) la *elektreetheedad*

electronic electrónico *elektroneeko*

email email (m) *eemayl*

to **email** hacer email *al eemayl*

to **embark** *(boat)* embarcar *embarkar*

embarrassing embarazoso/a *embarathoso/a*

embassy embajada (f) *embahhada*

emergency emergencia (f) *emerhhenthya*

emergency telephone teléfono de emergencia (m) *telefono de emerhhenthya*

empty vacío/a *batheeo/a*

to **empty** vaciar *bathyar*

enamel esmalte (m) *esmalte*

end fin (m) *feen*

to **end** terminar *termeenar*

energy energía (f) *enerhheea*

engaged *(to be married)* prometido/a *prometeedo/a (occupied)* ocupado/a *okoopado/a*

engine motor (m) *motor*

engineer ingeniero/a *inhhenyero/a*

England Inglaterra *eenglaterra*

English inglés/inglesa *eengles/eenglesa*

to **enjoy** disfrutar *desfrootar*

enough bastante *bastante*

to **enter** entrar *entrar*

entertainment entretenimiento (m) *entreteneemyento*

enthusiastic entusiasta (m/f) *entoosyasta*

entrance entrada (f) *entrada*

envelope sobre (m) *sobre*

environment medio ambiente (m) *medyo ambyente*

environmentally friendly ecológico *ekolohheeko*

equal igual *eegwal*

equipment equipo (m) *ekeepo*

escalator escalera mecánica (f) *eskalera mekaneeka*

especially especialmente *espethyalmente*

essential esencial *esenthyal*

estate agent agente inmobiliario (m) *ahhente eenmobeelyaryo*

even *(including)* hasta **as**ta *(not odd)* par *par*

evening tarde (f) *tarde*

every cada *kada*

everyone todo el mundo *todo el moondo*

everything todo *todo*

everywhere en todas partes *en todas partes*

exact, exactly exacto, exactamente *exakto, exaktamente*

examination examen (m) *examen*

example ejemplo (m) *ehhemplo*

» **for example** por ejemplo *por ehhemplo*

excellent excelente *exthelente*

except excepto *exthepto*

excess baggage exceso de equipaje (m) *extheso de ekeepahhe*

to exchange intercambiar *eenterkambyar* (money) cambiar *kambyar*

exchange rate tipo de cambio (m) *teepo de kambyo*

excited emocionado/a *emothyonado/a*

exciting emocionante *emothyonante*

excursion excursión (f) *exkoorsyon*

excuse me perdone *perdone*

executive (adj.) ejecutivo/a *ehhekooteebo/a*

exercise ejercicio (m) *ehhertheethyo*

exhibition exposición (f) *exposeethyon*

exit salida (f) *saleeda*

to expect esperar *esperar*

expensive caro/a *karo/a*

experience experiencia (f) *experyenthya*

experiment experimento (m) *expereemento*

expert experto/a *experto/a*

to explain explicar *expleekar*

explosion explosión (f) *explosyon*

export exportación (f) *exportathyon*

to export exportar *exportar*

express (train) expreso, rápido *expreso, rapeedo* (bus) directo *deerekto* (delivery) exprés *expres*

extension cable alargador (m) *alargador*

external externo/a *externo/a*

extra (in addition) aparte *aparte*

eye ojo (m) *ohho*

eyebrow ceja (f) *thehha*

eyelash pestaña (f) *pestanya*

eyeliner lápiz de ojos (m) *lapeeth de ohhos*

eyeshadow sombra de ojos (f) *sombra de ohhos*

F

fabric tela (f) *tela*

face cara (f) *kara*

face cream crema de belleza (f) *krema de belyetha*

face powder polvos para la cara (m/pl) *polbos para la kara*

facilities instalaciones (f/pl) *eenstalathyones*

fact hecho (m) *echo*
» **in fact** en realidad *en realeedad*

factory fábrica (f) *fabreeka*

to fail (exam/test) suspender *soospender*

failure fracaso (m) *frakaso*

to faint desmayarse *desmayarse*

fair (haired) rubio/a *roobyo/a*

fair feria (f) *ferya*

fairly bastante *bastante*

faith fe (f) *fe*

fake falso/a *falso/a*

to fall (down/over) caer *kaer*

false falso/a *falso/a* (teeth, etc.) postizo/a *posteetho/a*

familiar familiar *fameelyar*

family familia (f) *fameelya*

famous famoso/a *famoso/a*

fan (air) ventilador (m) *benteelador* (supporter) el/la hincha el/la *eencha*

fantastic fantástico/a *fantasteeko*

far (away) lejos *lehhos*

fare precio del billete (m) *prethyo del beelyete*

farm granja (f) *granhha*

farmer agricultor/a *agreekooltor/a*

fashion moda (f) *moda*

fashionable/in fashion a la moda *a la moda*

fast rápido/a *rapeedo/a*

fat (adj.) gordo/a *gordo/a* (noun) grasa (f) *grasa*

fatal mortal *mortal*

father padre (m) *padre*

father-in-law suegro (m) *swegro*

fault defecto (m) *defekto*

faulty defectuoso/a *defektwoso/a*

favourite favorito/a *faboreeto*

fax fax (m) *fax*

feather pluma (f) *plooma*

to be fed up estar harto/a *estar arto/a*

fee precio (m) *prethyo*

to **feed** dar de comer a *dar de komer a*
(baby) dar el pecho a *dar el pecho a*

to **feel** sentir *senteer* (ill/well) sentirse *senteerse*

female femenino/a *femeneeno/a*

feminist feminista (f) *femeeneesta*

ferry ferry (m) *ferree*

festival festival (m) *festeebal*

to **fetch** recoger *rekohher*

fever fiebre (f) *fyebre*

(a) few (unos) pocos *(oonos) pokos*

fiancé(e) novio/a *nobyo/a*

field campo (m) *kampo*

to **fight** pelear *pelear*

file (documents) archivo (m) *archeebo* (nail/DIY) lima (f) *leema*

to **fill** llenar *lyenar*

filling (dental) empaste (m) *empaste*

film película (f) *peleekoola*

filter filtro (m) *feeltro*

finance finanzas (f) *feenanthas*

to **find** encontrar *enkontrar*

fine (OK) vale *bale* (penalty) multa (f) *moolta* (weather) bueno/a *bweno/a*

finger dedo (m) *dedo*

to **finish** acabar *akabar*

fire fuego (m) *fwego*

fire brigade bomberos (m/pl) *bomberos*

fire extinguisher extintor (m) *exteentor*

firework fuegos artificiales (m/pl) *fwegos arteefeethyales*

firm firme *feerme*

firm (company) empresa (f) *empresa*

first primero/a *preemero/a*

first aid primeros auxilios *preemeros owxeelyos*

first aid kit botiquín (m) *boteekeen*

fish pez (m) *peth* (for eating) pescado (m) *peskado*

to **fish, to go fishing** pescar, ir a pescar *peskar, eer a peskar*

fishing rod caña de pescar (f) *canya de peskar*

fishmonger's pescadería (f) *peskadereea*

fit (healthy) en forma *en forma*

to **fit** ajustarse *ahhoostarse*

fitting room probador (m) *probador*

to **fix** (mend) arreglar *arreglar*

fizzy con gas *kon gas*

flag bandera (f) *bandera*

flash (camera) flash (m) *flash*

flat (apartment) piso (m) *peeso*

flat (level) llano/a *lyano/a* (battery, etc.) descargado/a *deskargado/a*

flavour sabor (m) *sabor*

flaw defecto (m) *defekto*

flea market rastro (m) *rastro*

flight vuelo (m) *bwelo*

flippers aletas (f) *aletas*

flood inundación (f) *inoondathyon*

floor suelo (m) *swelo*

» **on the first floor** en el primer piso *en el preemer peeso*

» **ground floor** planta baja (f) *planta bahha*

floppy disc disquete (m) *deeskete*

flour harina (f) *areena*

flower flor (f) *flor*

flu gripe (f) *greepe*

fluent (language) con fluidez *kon flweedeth*

fluid líquido (m) *leekeedo*

fly mosca (f) *moska*

fly sheet toldo impermeable (m) *toldo eempermeable*

fly spray insecticida (m) *eensekteetheeda*

to **fly** volar *bolar*

fog niebla (f) *nyebla*

foil papel de aluminio (m) *papel de aloomeenyo*

folding (e.g. chair) plegable *plegable*

folk music música folk (f) *mooseeka folk*

to **follow** seguir *segeer*

following (next) siguiente *seegyente*

food comida (f) *komeeda*

food poisoning intoxicación por alimentos (f) *eentoxeekathyon por aleementos*

foot pie (m) *pye*
» **on foot** a pie *a pye*

football fútbol (m) *footbol*

footpath sendero (m) *sendero*

for para, por *para, por*

forbidden prohibido/a *proeebeedo/a*

foreign, foreigner extranjero/a *extranhhero/a*

forest bosque (m) *boske*

to forget olvidar *olbeedar*

to forgive perdonar *perdonar*

fork tenedor (m) *tenedor*

form *(document)* formulario (m) *formoolaryo*

fortnight quincena (f) *keenthena*

fortress fortaleza (f) *fortaletha*

forward (hacia) adelante *(athya) adelante*

forwarding address dirección de reenvío (f) *deerekthyon de reenbeeo*

fountain fuente (f) *fwente*

fox zorro (m) *thorro*

foyer vestíbulo (m) *besteeboolo*

fracture fractura (f) *fraktoora*

fragile frágil *frahheel*

freckles pecas (f) *pekas*

free gratis *gratees (available/ unoccupied)* libre *leebre*

freedom libertad (f) *leebertad*

to freeze congelar *konhhelar*

freezer congelador (m) *konhhelador*

frequent frecuente *frekwente*

fresh fresco/a *fresko/a*

fridge nevera (f) *nebera*

fried frito/a *freeto/a*

friend amigo/a *ameego/a*

frightened asustado/a *asoostado/a*

frog rana (f) *rana*

from de, desde *de, desde*

front delante *delante*
» **in front of** delante de *delante de*

frontier frontera (f) *frontera*

frost helada (f) *elada*

frozen helado/a *elado/a*

fruit fruta (f) *froota*

to fry freír *fre-eer*

frying pan sartén (f) *sarten*

fuel carburante (m) *karboorante*

full lleno/a *lyeno/a*

full board pensión completa (f) *pensyon kompleta*

full up *(booked up)* completo/a *kompleto/a*

to have fun divertirse *deeberteerse*

funeral entierro (m) *entyerro*

funfair parque de atracciones (m) *parke de atrakthyones*

funny *(amusing)* divertido/a *deeberteedo/a (peculiar)* raro/a *raro/a*

fur pieles (f/pl) *pyeles*

furniture muebles (m) *mwebles*

further on más adelante *mas adelante*

fuse fusible (m) *fooseeble*

fusebox caja de fusibles (f) *kahha de fooseebles*

G

gallery galería (f) *galereea*

gambling juego (m) *hhwego*

game juego (m) *hhwego (match)* partido (m) *parteedo*

garage garaje (m) *garahhe (for parking)* cochera (f) *kochera (for petrol)* gasolinera (f) *gasoleenera*

garden jardín (m) *hhardeen*

gardener jardinero (m) *hhardeenero*

garlic ajo (m) *ahho*

gas gas (m) *gas*

gas bottle/cylinder bombona de gas (f) *bombona de gas*

gas refill cargador de gas (m) *kargador de gas*

gate puerta (f) *pwerta (airport)* puerta de embarque (f) *pwerta de embarke*

gay *(homosexual)* gay *gay*

gel *(hair)* gel (m) *hhel*

general general *hheneral*

» **in general** en general *en hheneral*

generous generoso/a *hheneroso/a*

gentle suave *swabe*

gentleman/men señor/es *senyor/es* (gents) caballeros *kabalyeros*

genuine genuino/a *hhenweeno/a*

German alemán/a *aleman/a*

Germany Alemania *alemanya*

to get obtener *obtener*

» **to get off** *(bus)* bajar *bahhar*

» **to get on** *(bus)* subir *soobeer*

» **to get through** *(phone)* comunicarse *komooneekarse*

gift regalo (m) *regalo*

gin ginebra (f) *hheenebra*

girl chica (f) *cheeka*

girlfriend novia (f) *nobya*

to give dar *dar*

to give back devolver *debolber*

glass vaso (m) *baso*

glasses gafas (f/pl) *gafas*

gloves guantes (m) *gwantes*

glue pegamento (m) *pegamento*

to go ir *eer*

» **to go away** irse *eerse*

» **to go down** bajar *bahhar*

» **to go in** entrar *entrar*

» **to go out** salir *saleer*

» **let's go!** ¡vamos! *bamos*

goal gol (m) *gol* (football) portería (f) *portereea*

goat cabra (f) *kabra*

God Dios (m) *dyos*

goggles gafas de bucear (f/pl) *gafas de boothear*

gold oro (m) *oro*

golf golf (m) *golf*

golf clubs palos de golf (m/pl) *palos de golf*

golf course campo de golf (m) *kampo de golf*

good bueno/a *bweno/a*

» **good evening** buenas tardes *bwenas tardes*

» **good morning** buenos días *bwenos deeas*

» **good night** buenas noches *bwenas noches*

goodbye adiós *adyos* (casual) hasta luego *asta lwego*

government gobierno (m) *gobyerno*

grammar gramática (f) *gramateeka*

gramme gramo (m) *gramo*

grandchildren nietos (m) *nyetos*

granddaughter nieta (f) *nyeta*

grandfather abuelo (m) *abwelo*

grandmother abuela (f) *abwela*

grandparents abuelos (m) *abwelos*

grandson nieto (m) *nyeto*

grass hierba (f) *yerba*

grateful agradecido/a *agradetheedo/a*

greasy grasiento/a *grasyento/a*

great! ¡estupendo! *estoopendo*

green verde *berde*

greengrocer's verdulería (f) *berdooleereea*

to greet saludar *saloodar*

grey gris *grees*

grilled a la parrilla *a la parreelya*

grocer's tienda de ultramarinos (f) *tyenda de ooltramareenos*

ground suelo (m) *swelo*

groundsheet tela impermeable (f) *tela eempermeable*

ground floor planta baja (f) *planta bahha*

group grupo (m) *groopo*

guarantee garantía (f) *garanteea*

guest invitado/a *eenbeetado/a*

guest house pensión (f) *pensyon*

guide guía (f) *geea*

guided tour visita con guía (f) *beeseeta kon geea*

guidebook guía (turística) (f) *geea (tooreesteeka)*

guilty culpable *koolpable*

guitar guitarra (f) *geetarra*

gun pistola (f) *peestola*

H

habit costumbre (f) *kostoombre*

hail granizo (m) *graneetho*

hair pelo (m) *pelo*

hairbrush cepillo (m) *thepeelyo*

haircut corte de pelo (m) *korte de pelo*

hairdresser peluquero/a *pelookero/a*

hairdryer secador de pelo (m) *sekador de pelo*

half mitad (f) *meetad*

half *(adj)* medio/a *medyo/a*

» **half board** media pensión (f) *medya pensyon*

» **half price** mitad de precio (f) *meetad de prethyo*

» **half an hour** media hora (f) *medeea ora*

» **half past** y media *ee medya*

hall *(in house)* vestíbulo (m) *besteeboolo*

ham jamón (m) *hhamon*

» **boiled ham** jamón York (m) *hhamon york*

» **cured ham** jamón serrano (m) *hhamon serrano*

hamburger hamburguesa (f) *amboorgesa*

hammer martillo (m) *marteelyo*

hand mano (f) *mano*

hand cream crema de manos (f) *krema de manos*

hand luggage equipaje de mano (m) *ekeepahhe de mano*

hand made hecho a mano *echo a mano*

handbag bolso (m) *bolso*

handkerchief pañuelo (m) *panywelo*

handle asa (m) *asa*

to hang up (telephone) colgar *kolgar*

hangover resaca (f) *resaka*

to happen pasar *pasar*

happy feliz *feleeth*

harbour puerto (m) *pwerto*

hard duro/a *dooro/a* *(difficult)* difícil *deefeetheel*

hard drive disco duro (m) *deesko dooro*

hard shoulder arcén (m) *arthen*

hardware shop ferretería (f) *ferreterya*

to hate odiar *odyar*

to have tener *tener*

hay heno (m) *eno*

hayfever fiebre del heno (f) *fyebre del eno*

he él *el*

head cabeza (f) *kabetha* *(boss)* jefe (m) *hhefe*

headache dolor de cabeza (m) *dolor de kabetha*

headphones cascos (m/pl) *kaskos*

to heal curar *koorar*

health salud (f) *salood*

healthy sano/a *sano/a*

health foods alimentos dietéticos (m/pl) *aleementos dyeteteekos*

to hear oír *oeer*

hearing oído (m) *oeedo*

hearing aid audífono (m) *owdeefono*

heart corazón (m) *korathon*

heart attack infarto (m) *eenfarto*

heat calor (m) *kalor*

heater calentador (m) *kalentador*

heating calefacción (f) *kalefacthyon*

heavy pesado/a *pesado/a*

heel tobillo (m) *tobeelyo* *(shoe)* tacón (m) *takon*

height altura (f) *altoora*

helicopter helicóptero (m) *eleekoptero*

hello hola *ola*

helmet *(motorbike)* casco (m) *kasko*

help ayuda (f) *ayooda*

help! ¡socorro! *sokorro*

to help ayudar *ayoodar*

her *(adj. and pronoun)* la, le, ella *la, le elya*

herb hierba (f) *yerba*

herbal tea infusión (f) *eenfoosyon*

here aquí *akee*

hers suyo/a *sooyo/a*

hiccups: to have hiccups hipo: tener hipo (m) *eepo: tener eepo*

high alto/a *alto/a*

high chair silla alta (f) *seelya alta*

to **hijack** secuestrar *sekwestrar*

hill colina (f) *koleena*

him lo, le, él *lo, le, el*

to **hire** alquilar *alkeelar*

his *(adj. and pronoun)* su, suyo/a *soo, sooyo/a*

history historia (f) *eestorya*

to **hit** pegar *pegar*

to **hitchhike** hacer autostop *ather owtostop*

HIV VIH (m) *oobe ee ache*

» **HIV positive** seropositivo/a *seroposeeteebo/a*

hobby pasatiempo (m) *pasatyempo*

to **hold** mantener *mantener*

hole agujero (m) *agoohhero*

holiday vacaciones (f) *bakathyones*

» **on holiday** de vacaciones *de bakathyones*

holy santo/a *santo/a*

home casa (f) *kasa*

» **at home** en casa *en kasa*

homeopathic homeopático *omeopateeko*

homosexual homosexual *omosexwal*

honest honesto/a *onesto/a*

honeymoon luna de miel (f) *loona de myel*

to **hope** esperar *esperar*

» **I hope so/not** espero que sí/no *espero ke see/no*

horrible horrible *orreeble*

horse caballo (m) *kabalyo*

hospital hospital (m) *ospeetal*

host anfitrión/anfitriona *anfeetryon/ anfeetryona*

hot caliente *kalyente* (spicy) picante *peekante*

hotel hotel (m) *otel*

hour hora (f) *ora*

house casa (f) *kasa*

housework tareas domésticas (f) *tareas domesteekas*

hovercraft aerodeslizador (m) *aerodesleethador*

how cómo *komo*

» **how far?** ¿cómo de lejos? *komo de lehhos*

» **how long?** ¿cuánto tiempo? *kwanto tyempo*

» **how many?** ¿cuántos/as? *kwantos/as*

» **how much?** ¿cuánto/a? *kwanto*

human humano/a *oomano/a*

hungry hambriento/a *ambryento/a*

» **to be hungry** tener hambre *tener ambre*

to **hunt** cazar *kathar*

hunting caza (f) *katha*

hurry: to be in a hurry prisa: tener prisa (f) *preesa: tener preesa*

to **hurt** doler *doler*

» **it hurts** duele *dwele*

husband marido (m) *mareedo*

hut cabaña (f) *kabanya*

hydrofoil aerodeslizador (m) *aerodesleethador*

I

I yo *yo*

ice hielo (m) *yelo*

ice rink pista de patinaje (f) *peesta de pateenahhe*

icy helado/a *elado/a*

idea idea (f) *eedea*

if si *see*

ill enfermo/a *enfermo/a*

illness enfermedad (f) *enfermedad*

to **imagine** imaginar *eemahheenar*

imagination imaginación (f) *eemahheenathyon*

immediately inmediatamente *eenmedyatamente*

immersion heater calentador de inmersión (m) *kalentador de eenmersyon*

important importante *eemportante*

impossible imposible *eemposeeble*

impressive impresionante *eempresyonante*

in en, dentro (de) *en, dentro (de)*

included incluido/a *eenklweedo/a*

independent independiente *eendependyente*

indigestion indigestión (f) *eendeehhestyon*

indoors dentro *dentro*

industry industria (f) *eendoostrya*

infected infectado/a *eenfektado/a*

infection infección (f) *eenfekthyon*

infectious infeccioso/a *eenfekthyoso/a*

inflamed inflamado/a *eenflamado/a*

influenza gripe (f) *greepe*

informal informal *eenformal*

information información (f) *eenformathyon*

information desk/office oficina de información (f) *ofeetheena de eenformathyon*

injection inyección (f) *eenyekthyon*

to injure herir *ereer*

injured herido/a *ereedo/a*

injury herida (f) *ereeda*

innocent inocente *eenothente*

insect insecto (m) *eensekto*

insect bite picadura (de insecto) (f) *peekadoora (de eensekto)*

insect repellent loción contra insectos (f) *lothyon kontra eensektos*

inside dentro (de) *dentro (de)*

to insist insistir *eenseesteer*

instant coffee café instantáneo (m) *kafe eenstantaneo*

instead of en vez de *en beth de*

instructor instructor (m) *eenstruktor*

insulin insulina (f) *eensooleena*

insult insulto (m) *eensoolto*

insurance seguro (m) *segooro*

» **insurance policy** póliza de seguro (f) *poleetha de segooro*

to insure asegurar *asegoorar*

insured asegurado/a *asegoorado/a*

intelligent inteligente *eenteleehhente*

interest *(money)* interés (m) *eenteres*

interested interesado/a *eenteresado/a*

interesting interesante *eenteresante*

international internacional *eenternathyonal*

Internet Internet (f) *eenternet*

Internet café cibercafé (m) *theeberkafe*

Internet connection conexión de Internet (f) *conexyon de eenternet*

to interpret interpretar *eenterpretar*

interpreter intérprete (m/f) *eenterprete*

interval *(theatre, etc.)* descanso (m) *deskanso*

interview entrevista (f) *entrebeesta*

into en *en*

to introduce presentar *presentar*

invitation invitación (f) *eenbeetathyon*

to invite invitar *eenbeetar*

iodine yodo (m) *yodo*

Ireland Irlanda *eerlanda*

Irish irlandés/irlandesa *eerlandes/eerlandesa*

iron *(metal)* hierro (m) *yerro* *(for clothes)* plancha (f) *plancha*

to iron planchar *planchar*

is (see also to be) es *es*

» **is/are there...?** ¿hay...? *iy...*

Islam Islam (m) *eeslam*

Islamic islámico/a *eeslamiko/a*

island isla (f) *eesla*

it lo/la *lo/la*

itch picor (m) *peekor*

J

jacket chaqueta (f) *chaketa*

jam mermelada (f) *mermelada*

jar tarro (m) *tarro*

jaw mandíbula (f) *mandeeboola*

jazz jazz (m) *yazz*

jeans vaqueros (m) *bakeros*

jelly gelatina (f) *hhelateena*

jellyfish medusa (f) *medoosa*

jetty embarcadero (m) *embarkadero*

jeweller's joyería (f) *hhoyereea*

Jewish judío/a *hhoodeeo/a*

job trabajo (m) *trabahho*

to **jog** hacer footing *ather footeeng*

jogging footing (m) *footeeng*

joke chiste (m) *cheeste*

journalist periodista (m/f) *peryodeesta*

journey viaje (m) *byahhe*

judge juez/a *hhweth/a*

jug jarra (f) *hharra*

juice zumo (m) *thoomo*

to **jump** saltar *saltar*

jump leads cables para cargar la batería (m) *kables para kargar la batereea*

jumper jersey (m) *hhersey*

junction (road) cruce (m) *kroothe*

just (only) solamente *solamente*

K

to **keep** guardar *gwardar* (to put by) conservar *konserbar*

kettle hervidor (m) *erbeedor*

key llave (f) *lyabe*

key ring llavero (m) *lyabero*

kidney riñón (m) *reenyon*

to **kill** matar *matar*

kilo(gram) kilo (m) *keelo*

kilometre kilómetro (m) *keelometro*

kind (sort) clase *klase* (generous) amable *amable*

king rey (m) *ray*

kiss beso (m) *beso*

to **kiss** besar *besar*

kitchen cocina (f) *kotheena*

knee rodilla (f) *rodeelya*

knickers bragas (f) *bragas*

knife cuchillo (m) *koocheelyo*

to **knock** golpear *golpear*

knot nudo (m) *noodo*

to **know** (someone) conocer *konother* (something) saber *saber*

» **I don't know** no sé *no se*

L

label etiqueta (f) *eteeketa*

ladder escalera (f) *eskalera*

lady señora (f) *senyora*

» **ladies** señoras (f/pl) *senyoras*

lager cerveza (f) *therbetha*

lake lago (m) *lago*

lamb (meat) cordero (m) *kordero*

lamp lámpara (f) *lampara*

lamp post farol (m) *farol*

land tierra (f) *tyerra*

to **land** aterrizar *aterreethar*

landlady propietaria (f) *propyetarya*

landlord propietario (m) *propyetaryo*

language idioma (m) *eedyoma*

large grande *grande*

last último/a *oolteemo/a*

to **last** durar *doorar*

late tarde (f) *tarde*

later más tarde *mas tarde*

laugh risa (f) *reesa*

to **laugh** reír *rayr*

launderette lavandería automática (f) *labandereea owtomateeka*

laundry colada (f) *kolada*

law ley (f) *lay*

lawyer abogado/a *abogado/a*

laxative laxante (m) *laxante*

lazy perezoso/a *perethoso/a*

lead plomo (m) *plomo*

» **lead-free** sin plomo *seen plomo*

leaf hoja (f) *ohha*

leaflet folleto (m) *folyeto*

to **lean** apoyarse *apoyarse*

to **learn** aprender *aprender*

learner estudiante (m/f) *estoodyante*

least: at least por lo menos *por lo menos*

leather piel (f) *pyel*

to **leave** dejar *dehhar* (to go away) marcharse *marcharse*

lecturer profesor universitario (m) _profesor ooneeberseetaryo_

left izquierdo/a _eethkyerdo/a_

left luggage _(office)_ consigna de equipajes (f) _konseegna de ekeepahhes_

leg pierna (f) _pyerna_

legal legal _legal_

lemon limón (m) _leemon_

lemonade limonada (f) _leemonada_

to **lend** prestar _prestar_

length longitud (f) _lonhheetood_

lens _(camera)_ objetivo (m) _obhheteebo_

lesbian lesbiana (f) _lesbyana_

less menos _menos_

lesson clase (f) _klase_

to **let** _(allow)_ permitir _permeeteer (rent)_ alquilar _alkeelar_

letter carta (f) _karta (of alphabet)_ letra (f) _letra_

letterbox buzón (m) _boothon_

lettuce lechuga (f) _lechooga_

leukemia leucemia (f) _lewthemya_

level _(height, standard)_ nivel (m) _neebel (flat)_ plano/a _plano/a_

level crossing paso a nivel (m) _paso a neebel_

library biblioteca (f) _beeblyoteka_

licence _(driving)_ carné de conducir (m) _carne de kondootheer (fishing, etc.)_ permiso de (m) _permeeso de_

lid tapa (f) _tapa_

to **lie down** echarse _echarse_

life vida (f) _beeda_

lifebelt cinturón salvavidas (m) _theentooron salbabeedas_

lifeboat bote salvavidas (m) _bote salbabeedas_

lifeguard el/la socorrista _el/la sokorreesta_

lifejacket chaleco salvavidas (m) _chaleko salbabeedas_

lift ascensor (m) _asthensor_

light luz (f) _looth_

light bulb bombilla (f) _bombeelya_

light _(coloured)_ claro/a _klaro/a (weight)_ ligero/a _leeheero/a_

to **light** _(fire)_ encender _enthender_

lighter _(cigarette)_ encendedor (m) _enthendedor_

lighter fuel líquido para encendedores (m) _leekeedo para enthendedores_

lightning relámpago (m) _relampago_

like _(similar to)_ como _komo_
  » **like this/that** así _asee_

to **like** _(food, people)_ gustar _goostar_
  » **I like** me gusta _me goosta_

likely probable _probable_

limited limitado/a _leemeetado/a_

line línea (f) _leenea_

lip labio (m) _labyo_

lipstick barra de labios (f) _barra de labyos_

liqueur licor (m) _leekor_

liquid líquido (m) _leekedo_

list lista (f) _leesta_

to **listen** escuchar _eskoochar_

litre litro (m) _leetro_

litter basura (f) _basoora_

little pequeño/a _pekenyo/a_
  » **a little** un poco (de) _oon poko (de)_

to **live** vivir _beebeer_

liver hígado (m) _eegado_

living-room salón (m) _salon_

loan préstamo (m) _prestamo_

local local _lokal_

lock cerradura (f) _therradoora_

to **lock** cerrar con llave _therrar kon lyabe_

locker armario (m) _armaryo_

London Londres _londres_

lonely solo/a _solo/a_

long largo/a _largo/a_

long-distance larga distancia _larga deestanthya_

long-distance call llamada a larga distancia (f) _lyamada a larga deestanthya_

look mirada (f) *meerada*
» **to look** (at) mirar *meerar*
» **to look for** buscar *booskar*
loose suelto/a *swelto/a*
lorry camión (m) *kamyon*
to **lose** perder *perder*
lost property office oficina de objetos
perdidos (f) *ofeeteena de obhhetos
perdeedos*
a lot (of) mucho/a *moocho/a*
lotion loción (f) *lothyon*
lottery lotería (f) *lotereea*
loud fuerte *fwerte*
lounge salón (m) *salon*
love amor (m) *amor*
to **love** querer *kerer*
low bajo *bahho*
low-fat bajo en grasas *bahho
en grasas*
lower más bajo *mas bahho*
luck: to be lucky suerte: tener suerte
swerte: tener swerte
luggage equipaje (m) *ekeepahhe*
lump (swelling) bulto (m) *boolto*
lunch el almuerzo (m) *el almwertho*

M

machine máquina (f) *makeena*
mad loco/a *loko/a*
madam señora (f) *senyora*
magazine revista (f) *rebeesta*
mail correo (m) *korreo*
main principal *preentheepal*
to **make** hacer *ather*
make-up maquillaje (m) *makeelyahhe*
male masculino/a *maskooleeno/a*
man hombre (m) *ombre*
to **manage** (cope) ser capaz *ser kapath*
manager gerente (m) *hherente*
many muchos/as *moochos/as*
» **not many** pocos/as *pokos/as*
map mapa (m) *mapa*
marble mármol (m) *marmol*
margarine margarina (f) *margareena*

market mercado (m) *merkado*
married casado/a *kasado/a*
» **to get married** casarse *kasarse*
mascara rímel (m) *reemel*
masculine masculino *maskooleeno*
mask máscara (f) *maskara*
mass (church) misa (f) *meesa*
match cerilla (f) *thereelya* (game)
partido (m) *parteedo*
material tela (f) *tela*
mathematics matemáticas (f)
matemateekas
matter: it doesn't matter no importa
no eemporta
» **what's the matter?** ¿qué pasa?
ke pasa
mattress colchón (m) *kolchon*
» **air mattress** colchón inflable (m)
kolchon eenflable
mature (cheese) curado *koorado*
me me, mí *me, mee*
meadow prado (m) *prado*
meal comida (f) *komeeda*
mean: what does this mean? ¿qué
significa? *ke seegneefeeka*
meanwhile mientras tanto *myentras
tanto*
measles sarampión (m) *sarampyon*
» **German measles** rubéola (f) *roobeola*
to **measure** medir *medeer*
measurement medida (f) *medeeda*
meat carne (f) *karne*
» **cold meats** embutidos (m/pl)
embooteedos
mechanic mecánico (m) *mekaneeko*
medical médico (m) *medeeko*
medicine (drug) medicamentos (m)
medeekamentos
medieval medieval *medyebal*
Mediterranean mediterráneo
medeeterraneo
medium (size) mediano/a *medyano/a*
(steak) medio/a *medyo/a* (wine)
semi-seco *semee-seko*

meeting reunión (f) *rewnyon*

member miembro (m) *myembro*

memory memoria (f) *memorya*

memory card *(for camera)* tarjeta de memoria (f) *tarhheta de memorya*

men hombres (m) *ombres*

to **mend** arreglar *arreglar*

menu *(à la carte)* carta (f) *karta* (set) menú (m) *menoo*

message mensaje (m) *mensahhe*

metal metal (m) *metal*

meter contador (m) *kontador*

metre metro (m) *metro*

microwave oven (horno) microondas (m) *(orno) meekro-ondas*

midday mediodía (m) *medyodeea*

middle centro (m) *thentro*

middle-aged mediana edad (f) *medyana edad*

midnight medianoche (f) *medyanoche*

migraine migraña (f) *meegranya*

mild suave *swabe*

mile milla (f) *meelya*

milk leche (f) *leche*

mill molino (m) *moleeno*

mind: do you mind if...? ¿le importa si...? *le eemporta see...*

» **I don't mind** no me importa *no me eemporta*

mine *(of me)* mío/a *meeo/a*

minibus minibús (m) *meeneeboos*

mini-disc minidisc (m) *meeneedeesk*

minister ministro/a *meeneestro/a*

minute minuto (m) *meenooto*

mirror espejo (m) *espehho*

Miss señorita (f) *senyoreeta*

to **miss** *(bus, etc.)* perder *perder* (nostalgia) echar de menos *echar de menos*

mist neblina (f) *nebleena*

mistake error (m) *error*

» **to make a mistake** cometer un error *kometer oon error*

mixed mixto/a *meexto/a*

mixture mezcla (f) *methkla*

mobile *(phone)* móvil (m) *mobeel*

model modelo (m) *modelo*

modem módem (m) *modem*

modern moderno/a *moderno/a*

moisturiser crema hidratante (f) *krema eedratante*

moment momento (m) *momento*

monastery monasterio (m) *monasteryo*

money dinero (m) *deenero*

month mes (m) *mes*

monthly mensual *menswal*

monument monumento (m) *monoomento*

moon luna (f) *loona*

moped ciclomotor (m) *theeklomotor*

more más *mas*

morning mañana (f) *manyana*

mortgage hipoteca (f) *eepoteka*

mosque mezquita (f) *methkeeta*

mosquito mosquito (m) *moskeeto*

mosquito net red para mosquitos (f) *red para moskeetos*

most (of) la mayor parte (de) *la mayor parte (de)*

mother madre (f) *madre*

mother-in-law suegra (f) *swegra*

motor motor (m) *motor*

motorbike moto(cicleta) (f) *moto(theekleta)*

motorboat lancha motora (f) *lancha motora*

motor racing carreras automovilísticas (f) *karreras owtomobeeleesteekas*

motorway autopista (f) *owtopeesta*

mountain montaña (f) *montanya*

mountaineering alpinismo (m) *alpeeneesmo*

mouse *(computer, animal)* ratón (m) *raton*

moustache bigote (m) *beegote*

mouth boca (f) *boka*

to **move** mover *mober*

Mr Sr (señor) (m) *senyor*

Mrs Sra (señora) (f) *senyora*

much mucho/a *moocho/a*

mug *(cup)* tazón (m) *tathon*

mullah ulema (m) *oolema*

to **murder** asesinar *aseseenar*

museum museo (m) *mooseo*

music música (f) *mooseeka*

musical musical (m) *mooseekal*

musician músico (m/f) *mooseeko*

Muslim musulmán *moosoolman*

must: you must tiene que *tyene ke*

my mi, mis *mee, mees*

mystery misterio (m) *meesteryo*

N

nail clavo (m) *klabo (finger/toe)* uña (f) *oonya*

» **nail clippers** cortaúñas (m/pl) *kortaoonyas*

» **nail file** lima de uñas (f) *leema de oonyas*

naked desnudo/a *desnoodo/a*

name nombre (m) *nombre*

napkin servilleta (f) *serbeelyeta*

nappy pañal (m) *panyal*

» **disposable nappy** dodotis (m) *dodotees*

national nacional *nathyonal*

nationality nacionalidad (f) *nathyonaleedad*

natural(ly) natural(mente) *natooral(mente)*

naughty travieso/a *trabyeso/a*

navy marina (f) *mareena*

navy blue azul marino (m) *athool mareeno*

near cerca (de) *therka (de)*

nearby cercano *therkano*

nearest más cercano *mas therkano*

nearly casi *kasee*

necessary necesario/a *nethesaryo/a*

necklace collar (m) *kolyar*

to **need** necesitar *netheseetar*

needle aguja (f) *agooha*

negative *(photo)* negativo (m) *negateebo*

neighbour vecino/a *betheeno/a*

neither ... nor ... ni ... ni... *nee ... nee...*

nephew sobrino (m) *sobreeno*

nervous nervioso/a *nerbyoso/a*

net red (f) *red*

never nunca *noonka*

new nuevo/a *nwebo/a*

New Year's Day Nochevieja (f) *nochebyehha*

news noticias (f/pl) *noteethyas*

newspaper periódico (m) *peryodeeko*

newspaper kiosk quiosco (m) *kyosko*

next siguiente *seegyente*

next to próximo/a a *proxeemo/a a*

nice *(person)* simpático/a *seempateeko/a (place)* bonito/a *boneeto/a*

niece sobrina (f) *sobreena*

night noche (f) *noche*

nightclub club (nocturno) (m) *cloob (noktoorno)*

nightdress camisón (m) *kameeson*

no no *no*

nobody nadie *nadye*

noise ruido (m) *rweedo*

noisy ruidoso *rweedoso*

non-alcoholic no alcohólico/a *no alkooleeko/a*

none ninguno/a *neengoono/a*

non-smoking no fumador *no foomador*

normal normal *normal*

normally normalmente *normalmente*

north norte (m) *norte*

nose nariz (f) *nareeth*

nosebleed hemorragia nasal (f) *emorrahheea nasal*

not no *no*

note *(bank)* billete (m) *beelyete*

notepad bloc (m) *blok*

nothing nada *nada*

» **nothing else** nada más *nada mas*

now ahora *aora*

nowhere en ninguna parte *en neengoona parte*

nuclear power energía nuclear (f) *enerhheea nooklear*

number número (m) *noomero*

nurse enfermero/a *enfermero/a*

nursery slope pista para principiantes (f) *peesta para preentheepyantes*

nut nuez (f) *nweth*

O

oar remo (m) *remo*

object *(thing)* objeto (m) *obhheto*

obvious obvio/a *obbyo/a*

occasionally de vez en cuando *de beth en kwando*

occupied ocupado/a *okoopado/a*

odd raro/a *raro/a (not even)* impar *eempar*

of de *de*

» **of course** por supuesto *por soopwesto*

off *(TV, light)* apagado/a *apagado/a (milk)* pasado/a *pasado/a*

offended ofendido/a *ofendeedo/a*

offer oferta (f) *oferta*

» **special offer** oferta especial (f) *oferta espethyal*

office oficina (f) *ofeetheena*

officer *(police)* agente (m) *ahhente*

official oficial *ofeethyal*

often muchas veces *moochas bethes*

» **how often?** ¿cuántas veces? *kwantas bethes*

oil aceite (m) *athayte*

OK vale *bale*

old viejo/a *byehho/a*

old-fashioned pasado/a de moda *pasado/a de moda*

olive aceituna (f) *athaytoona*

olive oil aceite de oliva (m) *athayte de oleeba*

on en *en (switched on)* encendido/a *enthendeedo*

once una vez *oona beth*

only solamente *solamente*

open abierto/a *abyerto/a*

to open abrir *abreer*

opera ópera (f) *opera*

operation operación (f) *operathyon*

opinion opinión (f) *opeenyon*

» **in my opinion** en mi opinión *en mee opeenyon*

opposite *(contrary)* contrario/a *kontraryo/a (position)* enfrente (de) *enfrente (de)*

optician el/la óptico *el/la opteeko*

or o *o*

orange *(fruit)* naranja (f) *naranhha (colour)* naranja (m) *naranhha*

order orden (f) *orden*

to order ordenar *ordenar*

ordinary ordinario/a *ordeenaryo/a*

to organise organizar *organeethar*

original(ly) original(mente) *oreehheenal(mente)*

other otro/a *otro/a*

our, ours nuestro/a *nwestro/a*

out (of) fuera (de) *fwera (de)*

outdoors, outside al aire libre *al iyre leebre*

over por encima de *por entheema de*

to overtake adelantar *adelantar*

to owe poseer *pose-er*

owner propietario/a *propyetaryo/a*

ozone-friendly que no daña la capa de ozono *ke no danya la kapa de othono*

ozone layer capa de ozono (f) *kapa de othono*

P

package tour viaje organizado (m) *byahhe organeethado*

packet paquete (m) *pakete*

paddle *(canoeing)* remo (m) *remo*

padlock candado (m) *kandado*

page página (f) *pahheena*

pain dolor (m) *dolor*

painful doloroso/a *doloroso/a*

painkiller calmante (m) *kalmante*

to paint pintar *peentar*

painter pintor/a *peentor/a*

painting cuadro (m) *kwadro*

pair par (m), pareja (f) *par, parehha*

palace palacio (m) *palathyo*

pale pálido/a *paleedo/a*

pants calzoncillos (m/pl) *kalthontheelyos*

paper papel (m) *papel*

paraffin parafina (f) *parafeena*

paralysed paralizado/a *paraleethado/a*

parcel paquete (m) *pakete*

pardon? ¿qué?, ¿cómo? *ke, komo*

parents padres (m/pl) *padres*

park parque (m) *parke*

to park aparcar *aparkar*

parking aparcamiento (m) *aparkamyento*

parking meter parquímetro (m) *parkeemetro*

parliament parlamento (m) *parlamento*

part parte (f) *parte*

particular: in particular en particular *en parteekoolar*

partly en parte *en parte*

partner (business) socio/a *sothyo/a*

party fiesta (f) *fyesta* (political) partido (m) *parteedo*

to pass (on road) cruzar *kroothar* (salt, etc) pasar *pasar* (test) aprobar *aprobar*

passenger pasajero/a *pasahhero/a*

passion pasión (f) *pasyon*

passport pasaporte (m) *pasaporte*

passport control control de pasaportes (m) *kontrol de pasaportes*

password contraseña (f) *kontrasenya*

past pasado (m) *pasado*
» in the past en el pasado *en el pasado*

pasta pasta (f) *pasta*

pastry pastel (m) *pastel*

path camino (m) *kameeno*

patient (hospital) paciente (m/f) *pathyente*

pattern diseño (m) *deesenyo*

pavement acera (f) *athera*

to pay pagar *pagar*
» to pay cash pagar al contado *pagar al kontado*

pay-as-you-go (phone) (teléfono) de tarjeta *telefono de tarhheta*

peace paz (f) *path*

peanut cacahuete (m) *kakawete*

pedal pedal (m) *pedal*

pedal-boat patín (m) *pateen*

pedestrian peatón (m) *peaton*

pedestrian crossing paso de peatones (m) *paso de peatones*

to peel pelar *pelar*

peg pinza (f) *peentha*

pen pluma (f) *plooma*

pencil lápiz (m) *lapeeth*

penknife navaja (f) *nabahha*

penicillin penicilina (f) *peneetheeleena*

pension pensión (f) *pensyon*

pensioner jubilado/a *hhoobeelado/a*

people gente (f) *hhente*

pepper pimienta (f) *peemyenta*
» green/red pepper pimiento verde/rojo (m) *peemyento berde/rohho*

per por *por*

perfect perfecto/a *perfekto/a*

performance representación (f) *representathyon*

perfume perfume (m) *perfoome*

perhaps quizás *keethas*

period (menstrual) regla (f) *regla*
» period pains dolores menstruales (m) *dolores menstrwales*

perm permanente (f) *permanente*

permit permiso (m) *permeeso*

to permit permitir *permeeteer*

personal personal *personal*

petrol gasolina (f) *gasoleena*

petrol can bidón de gasolina (m) *beedon de gasoleena*

petrol station gasolinera (f) *gasoleenera*

philosophy filosofía (f) *feelosofeea*

photocopy fotocopia (f) *fotokopya*

to photocopy fotocopiar *fotokopyar*

photo foto (f) *foto*

photographer fotógrafo/a *fotografo/a*

phrase book manual de conversación (m) *manwal de konbersathyon*

piano piano (m) *pyano*

to pick (choose) elegir *elehheer* (flowers, etc.) coger *kohher*

picnic merienda (f) *meryenda*

picture cuadro (m) *kwadro*

piece pedazo (m) *pedatho*

pier embarcadero (m) *embarkadero*

pig cerdo (m) *therdo*

pill píldora (f) *peeldora*

» **the pill** píldora anticonceptiva (f) *peeldora anteekonthepteeba*

pillow almohada (f) *almoada*

pillowcase funda de almohada (f) *foonda de almoada*

pilot piloto (m) *peeloto*

pilot light piloto (m) *peeloto*

pin alfiler (m) *alfeeler*

pink rosa *rosa*

pipe (smoking) pipa (f) *peepa* (drain) tubería (f) *toobereea*

place lugar (m) *loogar* (seat) asiento (m) *asyento*

plain sencillo *sentheelyo*

plan plano (m) *plano*

plane avión (m) *abyon*

plant planta (f) *planta*

plaster (sticking) tirita (f) *teereeta*

plastic plástico (m) *plasteeko*

plastic bag bolsa de plástico (f) *bolsa de plasteeko*

plate plato (m) *plato*

platform andén (m) *anden*

play (theatre) obra (de teatro) (f) *obra (de teatro)*

to play (game) jugar *hhoogar* (instrument) tocar *tokar*

pleasant agradable *agradable*

please por favor *por fabor*

pleased contento/a *kontento/a*

plenty (of) mucho (de) *moocho (de)*

plug (bath) tapón (m) *tapon* (electrical) enchufe (m) *enchoofe*

plumber fontanero (m) *fontanero*

pneumonia neumonía (f) *neoomoneea*

pocket bolsillo (m) *bolseelyo*

point punto (m) *poonto* (needle, pin) punta (f) *poonta*

poisonous venenoso/a *benenoso/a*

police policía (f) *poleetheea*

police car coche de policía (m) *koche de poleetheea*

police station comisaría (f) *komeesareea*

polish betún (m) *betoon*

polite cortés *kortes*

politician político/a *poleeteeko/a*

political político/a *poleeteeko/a*

politics política (f) *poleeteeka*

polluted contaminado/a *kontameenado/a*

pollution contaminación (f) *kontameenathyon*

pool (swimming) piscina (f) *peestheena*

poor pobre *pobre*

pop (music) música pop (f) *mooseeka pop*

Pope Papa (m) *papa*

popular popular *popoolar*

pork cerdo (m) *therdo*

port (harbour) puerto (m) *pwerto* (wine) oporto (m) *oporto*

portable portátil *portateel*

porter portero (m) *portero*

portion ración (f) *rathyon*

portrait retrato (m) *retrato*

positive (sure) segurísimo/a *segooreeseemo/a*

possible posible *poseeble*

» **as ... as possible** lo más ... posible *lo mas ... poseeble*

possibly posiblemente *poseeblemente*

post (mail) correo (m) *korreo*

to post enviar por correo *enbyar por korreo*
  postbox buzón (m) *boothon*
  postcard postal (f) *postal*
  postcode código postal (m) *kodeego postal*
  poster póster (m) *poster* (billboard) cartel (m) *kartel*
  postman/woman cartero/a (m/f) *kartero/a*
  post office oficina de correos (f) *ofeetheena de korreos*
to postpone aplazar *aplathar*
  pot olla (f) *olya*
  potato patata (f) *patata*
  pottery cerámica (f) *therameeka*
  potty *(child's)* orinal (m) *oreenal*
  pound *(sterling)* libra (esterlina) (f) *leebra (esterleena)*
to pour echar *echar*
  powder polvo (m) *polbo*
  powdered milk leche en polvo (f) *leche en polbo*
  power *(electrical)* corriente (f) *korryente* *(physical strength)* fuerza (f) *fwertha*
  power cut apagón (m) *apagon*
  pram cochecito (m) *kochetheeto*
to prefer preferir *prefereer*
  pregnant embarazada (f) *embarathada*
to prepare preparar *preparar*
  prescription receta (f) *retheta*
  present *(gift)* regalo (m) *regalo*
  press *(newspapers)* prensa (f) *prensa*
to press apretar *apretar*
  pretty bonito/a *boneeto/a*
  price precio (m) *prethyo*
  priest sacerdote (m) *satherdote*
  prime minister primer ministro (m/f) *preemer meeneestro*
  prince príncipe (m) *preentheepe*
  princess princesa (f) *preenthesa*
  print *(photo)* copia (f) *kopya*
to print imprimir *eempreemeer*
  prison cárcel (f) *karthel*
  private privado/a *preebado/a*

  prize premio (m) *premyo*
  probably probablemente *probablemente*
  problem problema (m) *problema*
  profession profesión (f) *profesyon*
  profit beneficio (m) *benefeethyo*
  programme programa (m) *programa*
  prohibited prohibido/a *proeebeedo/a*
to promise prometer *prometer*
to pronounce pronunciar *pronoonthyar*
  properly correctamente *korrektamente*
  property propiedad (f) *propyedad*
  protestant protestante *protestante*
  public público (m) *poobleeko* (adj.) público/a *poobleeko/a*
  public holiday día festivo (m) *deea festeebo*
to pull tirar *teerar*
to pump up inflar *eenflar*
  puncture pinchazo (m) *peenchatho*
  pure puro/a *pooro/a*
  purple morado/a *morado/a*
  purse monedero (m) *monedero*
to push empujar *empoohhar*
  push-chair sillita (f) *seelyeeta*
to put down poner *poner*
to put on *(clothes)* ponerse *ponerse*
  pyjamas pijama (m) *peehhama*

Q

  quality calidad (f) *kaleedad*
  quarter cuarto (m) *kwarto*
  quay muelle (m) *mwelye*
  queen reina (f) *rayna*
  question pregunta (f) *pregoonta*
  queue cola (f) *kola*
  quick(ly) rápida(mente) *rapeeda(mente)*
  quiet silencioso/a *seelenthyoso/a* *(place)* tranquilo/a *trankeelo/a*
  quite bastante *bastante*

R

  rabbi rabino (m) *rabeeno*
  rabbit conejo (m) *konehho*
  rabies rabia (f) *rabya*

racecourse pista de carreras (f) *peesta de karreras*

racing carreras (f/pl) *karreras*

racket *(tennis)* raqueta (f) *raketa*

radiator radiador (m) *radyador*

radio radio (f) *radyo*

radio station emisora (f) *emeesora*

radioactive radioactivo/a *radyoakteebo/a*

raft balsa (f) *balsa*

railway ferrocarril (m) *ferrocarreel*

railway station estación (de ferrocarril) (f) *estathyon (de ferrocarreel)*

rain lluvia (f) *lyoobya*
» **it's raining** está lloviendo *esta lyobyendo*

raincoat impermeable (m) *eempermeable*

rare raro/a **raro/a** *(steak)* poco hecho/a *poko echo/a*

rash *(spots)* sarpullido (m) *sarpoolyeedo*

rate *(speed)* velocidad (f) *belotheedad* *(tariff)* tarifa (f) *tareefa*

rather *(quite)* bastante *bastante*

raw crudo/a *kroodo/a*

razor maquinilla de afeitar (f) *makeeneelya de afaytar*

razor blade cuchilla de afeitar (f) *koocheelya de afaytar*

to reach llegar a *lyegar a*

to read leer *le-er*

reading lectura (f) *lektoora*

ready listo/a *leesto/a*

real *(authentic)* auténtico/a *owtenteeko/a*

really realmente *realmente*

rear trasero/a *trasero/a*

reason razón (f) *rathon*

receipt recibo (m) *retheebo*

receiver *(telephone)* auricular (m) *owreekoolar*

reception recepción (f) *rethepthyon*

receptionist recepcionista (f) *rethepthyoneesta*

recipe receta (f) *retheta*

to recognise reconocer *rekonother*

to recommend recomendar *rekomendar*

to recover *(from an illness)* recuperarse *rekooperarse*

red rojo/a *rohho/a*

Red Cross Cruz Roja (f) *krooth rohha*

reduction reducción (f) *redookthyon*

to refill rellenar *relyenar*

refrigerator nevera (f) *nebera*

refugee refugiado/a *refoohhyado/a*

refund reembolso (m) *re-embolso*

to refund reembolsar *re-embolsar*

region región (f) *rehhyon*

to register *(luggage, etc)* facturar *faktoorar*

registered *(letter)* certificada *therteefeekada*

registration number matrícula (f) *matreekoola*

registration document *(car)* documento de matriculación (m) *dokoomento de matreekoolathyon*

relation pariente/a *paryente/a*

relatively relativamente *relateebamente*

religion religión (f) *releehhyon*

to remain permanecer *permanether*

to remember recordar *rekordar*

to remove quitar *keetar* *(tooth)* sacar *sakar*

rent alquiler (m) *alkeeler*

to rent alquilar *alkeelar*

to repair reparar *reparar*

to repeat repetir *repeteer*

reply respuesta (f) *respwesta*

to reply responder *responder*

report informe (m) *eenforme*

to report *(crime)* denunciar *denoonthyar*

to rescue rescatar *reskatar*

reservation *(hotel, etc)* reserva (f) *reserba*

to reserve reservar *reserbar*

reserved reservado/a *reserbado/a*

responsible responsable *responsable*

to rest descansar *deskansar*

restaurant restaurante (m) *restowrante*

result resultado (m) *resooltado*

retired jubilado/a *hhoobeelado/a*

return vuelta (f) *bwelta (ticket)* ida y
vuelta *eeda ee bwelta*
to return volver *bolber (give back)* devolver
debolber
to reverse *(car)* dar marcha atrás *dar
marcha atras*
reverse-charge call llamada a cobro
revertido (f) *lyamada a kobro
reberteedo*
rheumatism reumatismo (m)
rwmateesmo
rice arroz (m) *arroth*
rich rico/a *reeko/a*
to ride *(horse/bike)* montar *montar*
right derecho/a *derecho/a (correct)*
correcto/a *korrekto/a*
» **to be right** tener razón *tener rathon*
right-hand derecho/a *derecho/a*
ring *(jewellery)* anillo (m) *aneelyo*
ripe maduro/a *madooro/a*
river río (m) *reeo*
road carretera (f) *karretera*
roadworks obras (f) *obras*
roast asado/a *asado/a*
to rob robar *robar*
robbery robo (m) *robo*
roof tejado (m) *tehhado*
room habitación (f) *abeetathyon
(space)* sitio (m) *seetyo*
rope cuerda (f) *kwerda*
rose rosa (f) *rosa*
rotten podrido/a *podreedo/a*
rough *(surface)* áspero/a
aspero/a (sea)
picado/a *peekado/a*
round redondo/a *redondo/a*
roundabout rotonda (f) *rotonda*
row *(theatre, etc.)* fila (f) *feela*
to row remar *remar*
rowing boat barca de remos (f) *barka de
remos*
royal real *real*
rubber goma (f) *goma*
rubbish basura (f) *basoora*

rucksack mochila (f) *mocheela*
rude grosero/a *grosero/a*
ruins ruinas (f) *rweenas*
ruler *(for measuring)* regla (f) *regla*
rum ron (m) *ron*
to run correr *korrer*
rush hour hora punta (f) *ora poonta*
rusty oxidado/a *oxeedado/a*

S

sad triste *treeste*
safe seguro/a *segooro/a (strongbox)* caja
fuerte (f) *kahha fwerte*
safety pin imperdible (m) *eemperdeeble*
sail vela (f) *bela*
to sail navegar *nabegar*
sailing vela (f) *bela*
sailing boat velero (m) *belero*
saint santo/a *santo/a*
salad ensalada (f) *ensalada*
sale *(bargains)* rebajas (f) *rebahhas*
salmon salmón (m) *salmon*
salt sal (f) *sal*
salty salado/a *salado/a*
same mismo/a *meesmo/a*
sample muestra (f) *mwestra*
sand arena (f) *arena*
sandals sandalias (f) *sandalyas*
sandwich bocadillo (m) *bokadeelyo
(toasted)* sandwich (m) *sanweech*
sandy arenoso/a *arenoso/a*
sanitary towels compresas (f) *kompresas*
sauce salsa (f) *salsa*
saucepan cacerola (f) *catherola*
saucer platillo (m) *plateelyo*
sauna sauna (f) *saoona*
to save *(money)* ahorrar *aorrar*
to say decir *detheer*
to scald escaldar *eskaldar*
scales báscula (f) *baskoola*
scarf bufanda (f) *boofanda (head)*
pañuelo (para la cabeza) (m)
panywelo (para la kabetha)
scene escena (f) *esthena*

scenery escenario (m) *esthenaryo*

scent aroma (m) *aroma*

school escuela (f) *eskwela*

science ciencia (f) *thyentheeya*

scientist científico (m) *thyenteefeeko*

scissors tijeras (f/pl) *teehheras*

scooter escúter (m) *eskooter*

score: what's the score? ¿cómo está el marcador? *komo esta el markador*

Scotland Escocia (f) *eskothya*

Scottish escocés/escocesa *eskothes/ eskothesa*

scratch arañazo (m) *aranyatho*

to scratch arañar *aranyar*

screen pantalla (f) *pantalya*

screw tornillo (m) *torneelyo*

screwdriver destornillador (m) *destorneelyador*

sculpture escultura (f) *eskooltoora*

sea mar (m) *mar*

seafood marisco (m) *mareesco*

seasick mareado/a *mareado/a*

season estación (f) *estathyon*

season ticket abono (m) *abono*

seat asiento (m) *asyento*

seatbelt cinturón de seguridad (m) *theentooron de segooreedad*

second (time period) segundo (m) *segoondo* (adj.) segundo/a *segoondo/a*

secret secreto (m) *sekreto*

section sección (f) *sekthyon*

sedative sedante (m) *sedante*

to see ver *ber*

to seem parecer *parether*

self-catering sin pensión *seen pensyon*

self-service autoservicio (m) *owtoserbeethyo*

to sell vender *bender*

to send enviar *enbyar*

senior citizen pensionista (m/f) *pensyoneesta*

sensible sensato/a *sensato/a*

sentence frase (f) *frase*

separate(d) separado/a *separado/a*

septic tank pozo negro (m) *potho negro*

serious serio/a *seryo/a* (grave) grave *grabe*

to serve servir *serbeer*

service (charge) servicio (m) *serbeethyo* (church) culto (m) *koolto*

several varios/as *baryos/as*

to sew coser *koser*

sex (gender) sexo (m) *sexo* (intercourse) relaciones sexuales (f) *relathyones sexwales*

shade (not sunny) sombra (f) *sombra*

shadow sombra (f) *sombra*

shampoo champú (m) *champoo*

sharp afilado/a *afeelado/a*

shave afeitado (m) *afaytado*

to shave afeitar *afaytar*

shaving cream/foam crema/espuma de afeitar (f) *krema/espooma de afaytar*

she ella *elya*

sheep oveja (f) *obehha*

sheet sábana (f) *sabana*

shelf estantería (f) *estantereea*

shell (egg, nut) cáscara (f) *kaskara*

shelter refugio (m) *refoohhyo*

shiny brillante *breelyante*

ship barco (m) *barko*

shirt camisa (f) *kameesa*

shock (electrical) descarga eléctrica (f) *deskarga elektreeka* (emotional) susto *soosto*

shocked horrorizado/a *orroreethado/a*

shoe(s) zapato(s) (m)(pl) *thapato(s)*

shoelace cordón (m) *kordon*

shoe polish betún de los zapatos (m) *betoon de los thapatos*

shoe shop zapatería (f) *thapatereea*

shop tienda (f) *tyenda*

shop assistant dependiente (m/f) *dependyente*

shopping: to go shopping ir de compras *eer de kompras*

shopping centre centro comercial (m) *thentro komerthyal*

short corto/a **korto/a**

shorts pantalones cortos (m/pl) pantalones **kortos**

shout gritar **greetar**

show espectáculo (m) espek**takooloo**

to **show** mostrar **mostrar**

shower ducha (f) **doocha**

to **shower** ducharse **doocharse**

to **shrink** encoger enko**hher**

shrunk encogido/a enko**hheedo/a**

shut cerrado/a **therrado/a**

to **shut** cerrar **therrar**

shutter (camera) obturador (m) obtoora**dor**

sick enfermo/a en**fermo/a**

» to be **sick** vomitar bom**eetar**

» to feel **sick** tener náuseas **tener** **nowseas**

sick bag bolsa para el mareo (f) **bolsa** **para** el ma**reo**

side lado (m) **lado**

sieve colador (m) kola**dor**

sight (vision) vista (f) **beesta** (tourist) monumentos (m/pl) mono**omentos**

sightseeing hacer turismo a**ther** too**reesmo**

sign señal (f) sen**yal**

to **sign** firmar feer**mar**

signal señal (f) sen**yal**

signature firma (f) **feerma**

silent silencioso/a seelen**thyoso/a**

silk seda (f) **seda**

silver plata (f) **plata**

SIM card tarjeta SIM (f) tar**hheta** sim

similar parecido/a (a) paree**theedo/a** (a)

simple sencillo/a sen**theelyo/a**

since desde **desde**

to **sing** cantar kan**tar**

single (room) individual eendeebee**dwal** (ticket) de ida de **eeda** (unmarried) soltero/a sol**tero/a**

sink fregadero (m) frega**dero**

sir señor (m) sen**yor**

sister hermana (f) er**mana**

sister-in-law cuñada (f) koon**yada**

to **sit** (down) sentarse sen**tarse**

size (clothes) talla (f) **talya** (shoes) número (m) **noomero**

skates (ice) patín (m) pa**teen** (roller) patín de ruedas (m) pa**teen** de **rwedas**

to **skate** patinar patee**nar**

ski esquí (m) es**kee**

to **ski** esquiar es**kyar**

skiing esquí (m) es**kee**

» **ski boots** botas de esquí (f/pl) **botas** de es**kee**

» **ski-lift** telesquí (m) teles**kee**

» **ski pole** palo de esquí (m) **palo** de es**kee**

» **ski-run/slope** pista de esquí (f) **peesta** de es**kee**

skimmed milk leche desnatada (f) **leche** desna**tada**

skin piel (f) pyel

skirt falda (f) **falda**

sky cielo (m) **thyelo**

to **sleep** dormir dor**meer**

sleeper/sleeping-car coche cama (m) **koche kama**

sleeping bag saco de dormir (m) **sako** de dor**meer**

sleeve manga (f) **manga**

slice rodaja (f) ro**dahha**

sliced en rodajas en ro**dahhas**

slim delgado/a del**gado/a**

slippery resbaladizo/a resbala**deetho/a**

slow(ly) lenta(mente) **lenta(mente)**

small pequeño/a pe**kenyo/a**

smell olor (m) **olor**

to **smell** oler (of) oler a **oler** a

smile sonrisa (f) son**reesa**

to **smile** sonreír sonri**yr**

smoke humo (m) **oomo**

to **smoke** fumar foo**mar**

smooth liso/a **leeso/a**

to **sneeze** estornudar estornoo**dar**

snorkel esnórkel (m) es**norkel**

snow nieve (f) **nyebe**

to snow nevar *nebar*
>> **it's snowing** está nevando *esta nebando*
    snow chains cadenas para la nieve (f) *kadenas para la nyebe*
    so así *asee* (therefore) por lo tanto *por lo tanto*
    soap jabón (m) *hhabon*
    sober sobrio/a *sobryo/a*
    socialism socialismo (m) *sothyaleesmo*
    sock calcetín (m) *kaltheteen*
    socket enchufe (m) *enchoofe*
    soft blando/a *blando/a*
    soft drink bebida no alcohólica (f) *bebeeda no alco-oleeka*
    software software (m) *softwer*
    soldier soldado (m) *soldado*
    sold out agotado/a *agotado/a*
    solicitor abogado/a *abogado/a*
    solid sólido/a *soleedo/a*
    some algunos/as *algoonos/as*
    somehow de alguna manera *de algoona manera*
    someone alguien *algyen*
    something algo *algo*
    sometimes a veces *a bethes*
    somewhere en algún lugar *en algoon loogar*
    son hijo (m) *eehho*
    song canción (f) *kanthyon*
    son-in-law yerno (m) *yerno*
    soon pronto *pronto*
>> **as soon as possible** lo más pronto posible *lo mas pronto poseeble*
    sore dolorido *doloreedo*
    sorry: I'm sorry lo siento *lo syento*
    sort clase (f) *klase*
    sound sonido (m) *soneedo*
    soup sopa (f) *sopa*
    sour agrio/a *agryo/a*
    south sur (m) *soor*
    souvenir recuerdo (m) *rekwerdo*
    space espacio (m) *espathyo*
    spade pala (f) *pala*

spanner llave inglesa (f) *lyabe eenglesa*
    spare disponible *deesponeeble*
    spare time tiempo libre (m) *tyempo leebre*
    spare tyre rueda de repuesto (f) *rweda de repwesto*
    sparkling espumoso/a *espoomoso/a*
to speak hablar *ablar*
    special especial *espethyal*
    special offer oferta especial (f) *oferta espethyal*
    specialist especialista (m/f) *espethyaleesta*
    speciality especialidad (f) *espethyaleedad*
    spectacles gafas (f/pl) *gafas*
    speed velocidad (f) *belotheedad*
    speed limit límite de velocidad (m) *leemeete de belotheedad*
to spend (money) gastar *gastar* (time) pasar *pasar*
    spice especia (f) *espethya*
    spicy picante *peekante*
    spirits (alcohol) licores (m/pl) *leekores*
    splinter astilla (f) *asteelya*
to spoil estropear *estropear*
    sponge (bath) esponja (f) *esponhha*
    spoon cuchara (f) *koochara*
    sport deporte (m) *deporte*
    spot grano (m) *grano* (place) sitio (m) *sityo*
to sprain torcer *torther*
    sprained torcido/a *tortheedo/a*
    spray aerosol (m) *aerosol*
    spring (season) primavera (f) *preemabera*
    square plaza (f) *platha* (shape) cuadrado/a *kwadrado/a*
    stadium estadio (m) *estadyo*
    stain mancha (f) *mancha*
    stairs escaleras (f/pl) *eskaleras*
    stalls (theatre) butacas (f/pl) *bootakas*
    stamp (postage) sello (m) *selyo*
    stand (stadium) gradas (f/pl) *gradas*

193

to **stand up** levantarse *lebantarse*

stapler grapadora (f) *grapadora*

star estrella (f) *estrelya*

start comienzo (m) *komyentho*

to **start** comenzar *komenthar*

starter *(food)* entremés (m) *entremes*

state estado (m) *estado*

station estación (f) *estathyon*

stationer's papelería (f) *papelereea*

statue estatua (f) *estatwa*

to **stay** *(live)* alojarse *alohharse* *(remain)* quedarse *kedarse*

to **steal** robar *robar*

steam vapor (m) *bapor*

steamer barco de vapor (m) *barko de bapor*

steel acero (m) *athero*

steep empinado/a *empeenado/a*

step *(footstep)* paso (m) *paso* *(stairs)* peldaño (m) *peldanyo*

step-brother hermanastro (m) *ermanastro*

step-children hijastros (m/pl) *eehhastros*

step-father padrastro (m) *padrastro*

step-mother madrastra (f) *madrastra*

step-sister hermanastra (f) *ermanastra*

stereo estéreo (m) *estereo*

stick palo (m) *palo*

sticky pegajoso/a *pegahhoso/a*

sticky tape cinta adhesiva (f) *theenta adeseeba*

stiff rígido/a *reehheedo/a*

still *(yet)* todavía *todabeea*

still *(non-fizzy)* sin gas *seen gas*

sting picadura (f) *peekadoora*

to **sting** picar *peekar*

stock exchange bolsa (f) *bolsa*

stockings medias (f/pl) *medyas*

stolen robado/a *robado/a*

stomach estómago (m) *estomago*

stomach ache dolor de estómago (m) *dolor de estomago*

stomach upset trastorno estomacal (m) *trastorno estomakal*

stone piedra (f) *pyedra*

stop *(bus)* parada (f) *parada*

to **stop** parar *parar*

» **stop!** ¡alto! *alto*

stopcock llave de paso (f) *lyabe de paso*

story historia (f) *eestorya*

stove cocina (f) *kotheena*

straight derecho/a *derecho/a*

straight on todo recto *todo rekto*

strange extraño/a *extranyo/a*

stranger desconocido/a *deskonotheedo/a*

strap correa (f) *korrea*

straw *(drinking)* pajita (f) *pahheeta*

stream arroyo (m) *arroyo*

street calle (f) *kalye*

stretcher camilla (f) *kameelya*

strike huelga (f) *welga*

» **on strike** en huelga *en welga*

string cuerda (f) *kwerda*

stripe raya (f) *raya*

striped a rayas *a rayas*

strong fuerte *fwerte*

to **stick: it's stuck** está atascado *esta ataskado*

student estudiante (m/f) *estoodyante*

studio *(radio/TV)* estudio (m) *estoodyo*

to **study** estudiar *estoodyar*

stupid estúpido/a *estoopeedo/a*

style estilo (m) *esteelo*

subtitles subtítulos (m/pl) *soobteetoolos*

suburb suburbio (m) *sooboorbyo*

success éxito (m) *exeeto*

such tal *tal*

suddenly de repente *de repente*

sugar azúcar (m) *athookar*

sugar lump terrón de azúcar (m) *terron de athookar*

suit *(man's)* traje (m) *trahhe*

suitcase maleta (f) *maleta*

summer verano (m) *berano*

sun sol (m) *sol*

to **sunbathe** tomar el sol *tomar el sol*

sunburn quemadura de sol (f) *kemadoora de sol*

sunglasses gafas de sol (f/pl) *gafas de sol*

sunny soleado/a *soleado/a*

sunshade sombrilla (f) *sombreelya*

sunstroke insolación (f) *eensolathyon*

suntan bronceado/a *brontheado/a*

suntan lotion loción bronceadora (f) *lothyon brontheadora*

suntan oil aceite bronceador (m) *athayte brontheador*

supermarket supermercado (m) *soopermerkado*

supper cena (f) *thena*

supplement suplemento (m) *sooplemento*

suppose: I suppose so/not supongo que sí/no *soopongo ke see/no*

suppository supositorio (m) *sooposeetoryo*

sure seguro/a *segooro/a*

surface superficie (f) *sooperfeethye*

surname apellido (m) *apelyeedo*

surprise sorpresa (f) *sorpresa*

surprised sorprendido/a *sorprendeedo/a*

surrounded by rodeado/a de *rodeado/a de*

to sweat sudar *soodar*

sweatshirt sudadera (f) *soodadera*

to sweep barrer *barrer*

sweet dulce (m) *doolthe*

sweetener sacarina (f) *sakareena*

sweets caramelos (m/pl) *karamelos*

swelling hinchazón (f) *eenchathon*

to swim nadar *nadar*

swimming natación (f) *natathyon*

swimming pool piscina (f) *peestheena*

swimming trunks/swimsuit traje de baño (m) *trahhe de banyo*

switch interruptor (m) *eenterrooptor*

to switch off apagar *apagar*

to switch on encender *enthender*

swollen hinchado/a *eenchado/a*

symptom síntoma (m) *seentoma*

synagogue sinagoga (f) *seenagoga*

synthetic sintético/a *seentetiko/a*

system sistema (m) *seestema*

T

table mesa (f) *mesa*

tablet pastilla (f) *pasteelya*

table tennis ping-pong (m) *peen-pon*

tailor sastre (m) *sastre*

to take tomar *tomar* (photo) sacar *sakar* (time) tardar *tardar*

taken (seat) ocupado/a *okoopado/a*

to take off (clothes) quitarse *keetarse* (plane) despegar *despegar*

talcum powder polvos de talco (m) *polbos de talko*

to talk hablar *ablar*

tall alto/a *alto/a*

tampons tampones (m/pl) *tampones*

tap grifo (m) *greefo*

tape cinta (f) *theenta*

tape measure cinta métrica (f) *theenta metreeka*

taste sabor (m) *sabor*

to taste probar *probar*

tax impuesto (m) *eempwesto*

taxi taxi (m) *taxee*

taxi rank parada de taxis (f) *parada de taxees*

tea té (m) *te*

teabag bolsita de té (f) *bolseeta de te*

to teach enseñar *ensenyar*

teacher profesor/a *profesor/a*

team equipo (m) *ekeepo*

tear (cry) lágrima (f) *lagreema*

tear (rip) rasgar *rasgar*

teaspoon cucharilla (f) *koochareelya*

teat (for baby's bottle) tetilla (f) *teteelya*

tea-towel paño de cocina (m) *panyo de kotheena*

technical técnico/a *tekneeko/a*

technology tecnología (f) *tethnolohheea*

teenager adolescente (m/f) *adolesthente*

telegram telegrama (m) *telegrama*

telephone teléfono (m) *telefono*

telephone card tarjeta telefónica (f) *tarhheta telefoneeka*

telephone directory guía telefónica (f) ***gee**a telefo**nee**ka*

to telephone llamar por teléfono *l**ya**mar por te**le**fono*

television televisión (f) *telebee**syon***

to tell decir *de**theer***

temperature temperatura (f) *tempera**too**ra*

» **to have a temperature** tener fiebre *tener **fye**bre*

temporary provisional *probeesyo**nal***

tender tierno/a *t**yer**no/a*

tennis tenis (m) *te**nees***

tennis court pista de tenis (f) *p**ees**ta de te**nees***

tent tienda de campaña (f) *t**yen**da de kam**pa**nya*

tent peg estaca (f) *es**ta**ka*

tent pole palo (m) *palo*

terminal *(airport)* terminal (f) *termee**nal***

terminus estación terminal (f) *esta**thyon** termee**nal***

terrace terraza (f) *te**rra**tha*

terrible terrible *te**rree**ble*

terrorist terrorista (m/f) *terro**rees**ta*

to text enviar un mensaje de texto *en**byar** oon men**sahhe** de **tex**to*

text message mensaje de texto (m) *men**sahhe** de **tex**to*

than que *ke*

thank you (very much) (muchas) gracias (*moo**chas***) *gra**thyas***

that (one) ése/a, eso *ese/a, eso*

the el, la, los, las *el, la, los, las*

theatre teatro (m) *te**atro***

their su, sus *soo, soos*

theirs suyo/a, suyos/as *soo**yo**/a, soo**yos**/as*

them los/las, ellos/as *los/las, **el**yos/as*

then entonces *en**ton**thes* (later) después *des**pwes***

there allí *al**lee***

there is/are hay *iy*

therefore por lo tanto *por lo **tan**to*

thermometer termómetro (m) *ter**mo**metro*

these estos/as *es**tos**/as*

they ellos/as *el**yos**/as*

thick grueso/a *gr**we**so/a*

thief ladrón/ladrona *la**dron**/la**dro**na*

thin delgado/a *del**ga**do/a*

thing cosa (f) *ko**sa***

to think pensar *pen**sar*** (believe) creer *kre-**er***

third tercero/a *ter**the**ro/a*

thirsty: to be thirsty tener sed *tener sed*

this (one) éste/a, esto *este/a, esto*

those esos/as, aquellos/as *esos/as, ake**lyos**/as*

thread hilo (m) *ee**lo***

throat lozenges pastillas para la garganta (f) *pas**teel**yas para la gar**gan**ta*

through por *por*

to throw lanzar *lan**thar***

to throw away echar *e**char***

thumb pulgar (m) *pool**gar***

thunder trueno (m) *tr**we**no*

ticket *(travel)* billete (m) *beel**ye**te* (theatre, etc.) entrada (f) *en**tra**da*

ticket office taquilla (f) *ta**kee**lya*

tide *(high/low)* marea (f) *ma**re**a*

tidy ordenado/a *orde**na**do/a*

tie corbata (f) *kor**ba**ta*

to tie atar *a**tar***

tight *(clothes)* ajustado/a *ahhoos**ta**do/a*

tights medias (f/pl) *me**dyas***

till *(until)* hasta *a**sta***

time tiempo (m) *t**yem**po* (on clock) hora (f) *o**ra***

timetable *(train)* horario (m) *o**ra**ryo*

tin lata (f) *la**ta***

tin foil papel de aluminio (m) *pa**pel** de aloo**mee**nyo*

tin opener abrelatas (m) *abre**la**tas*

tinned en lata *en la**ta***

tip *(in restaurant)* propina (f) *pro**pee**na*

tired cansado/a *kan**sa**do/a*

tissues pañuelos de papel (m/pl) *panywelos de papel*

to a *a*

toast tostada (f) *tostada*

tobacco tabaco (m) *tabako*

tobacconist's estanco (m) *estanko*

toboggan tobogán (m) *tobogan*

today hoy *oy*

toiletries artículos de perfumería (m/pl) *arteekoolos de perfoomereea*

toilets servicios (m/pl) *serbeethyos*

toilet paper papel higiénico (m) *papel eehhyeneeko*

token ficha (f) *feecha*

toll peaje (m) *peahhe*

tomato tomate (m) *tomate*

tomorrow mañana *manyana*

tongue lengua (f) *lengwa*

tonight esta noche *esta noche*

too demasiado *demasyado*
    (as well) también *tambyen*

tool herramienta (f) *erramyenta*

tooth diente (m) *dyente*

toothache dolor de muelas (m) *dolor de mwelas*

toothbrush cepillo de dientes (m) *thepeelyo de dyentes*

toothpaste pasta de dientes (f) *pasta de dyentes*

toothpick palillo (m) *paleelyo*

top *(mountain)* cima (f) *theema*
  » **on top of** sobre, encima (de) *sobre, entheema (de)*

torch linterna (f) *leenterna*

torn rasgado/a *rasgado/a*

total total (m) *total*

totally totalmente *totalmente*

to touch tocar *tokar*

tough *(meat)* duro/a *dooro/a*

tour excursión (f) *exkoorsyon*

to tour viajar *byahhar*

tourism turismo (m) *tooreesmo*

tourist turista (m/f) *tooreesta*

tourist office oficina de turismo (f) *ofeetheena de tooreesmo*

to tow remolcar *remolkar*

towards hacia *athya*

towel toalla (f) *toalya*

tower torre (f) *torre*

town ciudad (f) *thyoodad*

town centre centro de la ciudad (m) *thentro de la thyoodad*

town hall ayuntamiento (m) *ayoontamyento*

toy juguete (m) *hhoogete*

track camino (m) *kameeno*

tracksuit chándal (m) *chandal*

traditional tradicional *tradeethyonal*

traffic tráfico (m) *trafeeko*

traffic jam embotellamiento (m) *embotelyamyento*

traffic light semáforo (m) *semaforo*

trailer remolque (m) *remolke*

train tren (m) *tren*
  » **by train** en tren *en tren*

trainers zapatillas de deporte (f/pl) *thapateelyas de deporte*

tram tranvía (m) *tranbeea*

tranquilliser tranquilizante (m) *trankeeleethante*

to translate traducir *tradootheer*

translation traducción (f) *tradookthyon*

to travel viajar *byahhar*

travel agency agencia de viajes (f) *ahhenthya de byahhes*

traveller's cheques cheques de viaje (m/pl) *chekes de byahhe*

travel sickness mareo (m) *mareo*

tray bandeja (f) *bandehha*

treatment tratamiento (m) *tratamyento*

tree árbol (m) *arbol*

trip viaje (m) *byahhe*

trousers pantalones (m/pl) *pantalones*

trout trucha (f) *troocha*

true verdad (f) *berdad*
  » **that's true** es verdad *es berdad*

to try intentar *eententar*

to try on probarse *probarse*

T-shirt camiseta (f) *kameeseta*

tube *(pipe)* tubo (m) *toobo*
  (underground) metro (m) *metro*

tuna atún (m) *atoon*

tunnel tunel (m) *toonel*

turn: it's my turn me toca *me toka*

to turn girar *hheerar*

to turn off apagar *apagar*

turning *(side road)* bocacalle (f)
  bokakalye

twice dos veces *dos bethes*

twin beds dos camas (f) *dos kamas*

twins gemelos/as *hhemelos/as*

twisted *(ankle)* torcido/a *tortheedo/a*

type *(sort)* tipo (m) *teepo*

typical típico/a *teepeeko/a*

U

UBS lead cable UBS (m) *kable oo be ese*

ugly feo/a *feo/a*

ulcer úlcera (f) *oolthera*

umbrella paraguas (m) *paragwas*

uncle tío (m) *teeo*

uncomfortable incómodo/a
  eenkomodo/a

under debajo de *debahho de*

underground *(tube)* metro (m) *metro*

underpants calzoncillos (m/pl)
  kalthontheelyos

underpass paso subterráneo (m) *paso
  soobterraneo*

to understand entender *entender*

underwater submarino/a *soobmareeno/a*

underwear ropa interior (f) *ropa eenteryor*

to undress desvestirse *desbesteerse*

unemployed en paro *en paro*

unfortunately desgraciadamente
  desgrathyadamente

unhappy infeliz *eenfeleeth*

uniform uniforme (m) *ooneeforme*

university universidad (f)
  ooneeberseedad

unleaded petrol gasolina sin plomo (f)
  gasoleena seen plomo

unless a menos que *a menos ke*

unpack deshacer la maleta *desather la
  maleta*

unpleasant desagradable *desagradable*

to unscrew destornillar *destorneelyar*

until hasta *asta*

unusual insólito/a *eensoleeto/a*

unwell enfermo/a *enfermo/a*

up arriba *arreeba*

uphill cuesta arriba *kwesta arreeba*

up the road por la carretera *por la
  karretera*

upper de arriba *de arreeba*

upstairs arriba *arreeba*

urgent urgente *oorhhente*

urine orina (f) *oreena*

us nosotros/as *nosotros/as*

to use usar *oosar*

useful útil *ooteel*

useless inútil *eenooteel*

usually normalmente *normalmente*

V

vacant libre *leebre*

vacuum cleaner aspiradora (f)
  aspeeradora

valid válido/a *baleedo/a*

valley valle (m) *balye*

valuable de valor de *balor*

valuables objetos de valor (m/pl)
  obhhetos de balor

van furgoneta (f) *foorgoneta*

vanilla vainilla (f) *biyneelya*

vase jarrón (m) *hharron*

VAT IVA (m) *eeba*

vegan vegano/a *begano/a*

vegetables verduras (f) *berdooras*

vegetarian vegetariano/a *behhetaryano/a*

vehicle vehículo (m) *be-eekoolo*

very muy *mwee*

vest camiseta (f) *kameeseta*

vet veterinario (m) *betereenaryo*

via por *por*
video vídeo (m) *beedeo*
view vista (f) *beesta*
villa chalet (m) *chale*
village pueblo (m) *pweblo*
vinegar vinagre (m) *beenagre*
vineyard viñedo (m) *beenyedo*
virgin virgen (f) *beerhhen*
visa visado (m) *beesado*
visit visita (f) *beeseeta*
to visit visitar *beeseetar*
visitor visitante (m/f) *beeseetante*
vitamin vitamina (f) *beetameena*
voice voz (f) *both*
volleyball voleibol (m) *boliybol*
voltage voltaje (m) *boltahhe*
to vote votar *botar*

W

wage sueldo (m) *sweldo*
waist cintura (f) *theentoora*
waistcoat chaleco (m) *chaleko*
to wait (for) esperar *esperar*
waiter camarero (m) *kamarero*
waiting room sala de espera
    (f) *sala de espera*
waitress camarera (f) *kamarera*
Wales Gales (m) *gales*
walk paseo (m) *paseo*
to walk, go for a walk caminar, ir de paseo
    kameenar, *eer de paseo*
walking stick bastón (m) *baston*
wall (inside) pared (f) *pared* (outside)
    muro (m) *mooro*
wallet cartera (f) *kartera*
to want querer *kerer*
war guerra (f) *gerra*
warm caliente *kalyente*
to wash lavar *labar*
washable lavable *labable*
wash-basin lavabo (m) *lababo*
washing lavado (m) *labado*
washing machine lavadora
    (f) *labadora*

washing powder detergente (m)
    deterhhente
to wash-up fregar los platos *fregar los platos*
washing-up liquid lavavajillas (m)
    lababahheelyas
wastepaper basket papelera (f) *papelera*
watch (clock) reloj (m) *relohh*
to watch mirar *meerar*
water (el) agua (f) *(el) agwa*
water heater calentador del agua (m)
    kalentador del agwa
waterfall cascada (f) *kaskada*
waterproof impermeable *eempermeable*
water-skiing esquí acuático (m) *eskee
    akwateeko*
water-skis esquís acuáticos (m) *eskees
    akwateekos*
wave ola (f) *ola*
way (path) camino (m) *kameeno*
wax cera (f) *thera*
we nosotros/as *nosotros/as*
weather tiempo (m) *tyempo*
weather forecast pronóstico del tiempo
    (m) *pronosteeko del tyempo*
web (Internet) web *web*
wedding boda (f) *boda*
week semana (f) *semana*
weekday día de la semana (m) *deea de
    la semana*
weekend fin de semana (m) *feen de
    semana*
weekly semanal *semanal*
to weigh pesar *pesar*
weight peso (m) *peso*
well (water) pozo (m) *potho*
well (adv.) bien *byen*
well done (steak) muy hecho/a *mwee
    echo/a*
Welsh galés/galesa *gales/galesa*
west oeste (m) *oeste*
western occidental *oktheedental*
wet mojado/a *mohhado/a*
wetsuit traje de bucear (m) *trahhe de
    boothear*

what que *ke*

what? ¿qué? *ke*

wheel rueda (f) *rweda*

wheelchair silla de ruedas (f) *seelya de rwedas*

when cuando *kwando*

when? ¿cuándo? *kwando*

where donde *donde*

where? ¿dónde? *donde*

which el/la/lo cual *el/la/lo kwal*

which? ¿qué?, ¿cuál?/¿cuáles? *ke, kwal/kwales*

while mientras *myentras*

white blanco/a *blanko/a*

who que *ke*

who? ¿quién? *kyen*

whole entero/a *entero/a*

why? ¿por qué? *por ke*

wide ancho/a *ancho/a*

widow viuda (f) *byooda*

widower viudo (m) *byoodo*

wife mujer (f) *moohher*

wild salvaje *salbahhe*

to win ganar *ganar*

wind viento (m) *byento*

windmill molino de viento (m) *moleeno de byento*

window ventana (f) *bentana (shop)* escaparate (m) *eskaparate*

to windsurf hacer windsurf *ather weensoorf*

windy: it's windy hace viento *athe byento*

wine vino (m) *beeno*

wine merchant bodega (f) *bodega*

wing (el) ala (f) *(el) ala*

winter invierno (m) *eenbyerno*

with con *kon*

without sin *seen*

woman mujer (f) *moohher*

wonderful maravilloso/a *marabeelyoso/a*

wood madera (f) *madera*

wool lana (f) *lana*

word palabra (f) *palabra*

work trabajo (m) *trabahho*

to work (job) trabajar *trabahhar (function)*

funcionar *foonthyonar*

world (noun) mundo (m) *moondo (adj.)* mundial *moondyal*

worried preocupado/a *preokoopado/a*

worse peor *peor*

worth: it's worth... vale... *bale...*

» **it's not worth it** no vale la pena *no bale la pena*

wound herida (f) *ereeda*

to wrap (up) envolver *enbolber*

wrong equivocado/a *ekeebokado/a*

to write escribir *eskreebeer*

writer escritor (m) *eskreetor*

writing paper papel de escribir (m) *papel de eskreebeer*

X

X-ray radiografía (f) *radyografeea*

Y

yacht yate (m) *yate*

to yawn bostezar *bostethar*

year año (m) *anyo*

yellow amarillo/a *amareelyo/a*

yes sí *see*

yesterday ayer *ayer*

yet todavía *todabeea*

yoghurt yogur (m) *yogoor*

you (formal) usted/ustedes *oosted/oostedes (informal sing.)* tú *too (informal pl.)* vosotros/as *bosotros/as*

young jóven *hhoben*

your (formal) su *soo*

your (informal, sing.) tu *(informal, pl.)* vuestro/a *too, bwestro/a*

yours suyo/a, tuyo/a, vuestro/a *sooyo/a, tooyo/a, bwestro/a*

youth juventud (f) *hoobentood*

youth hostel albergue de juventud (m) *alberge de hhobentood*

Z

zip cremallera (f) *kremalyera*

zoo zoo (m) *tho-o*

Spanish – English dictionary

A

a to, at
- a las... at... o'clock

abajo down, downstairs, below
- de abajo lower, bottom

abierto/a open
abogado (m) lawyer
abono (m) season ticket
aborto espontáneo (m) miscarriage
abrazo (m) hug
- » un (fuerte) abrazo, abrazos best wishes, regards

abrebotellas (m) bottle opener
abrelatas (m) tin/can opener
abrigo (m) coat
abrir to open
absoluto: en absoluto absolutely not, not at all
abuela (f) grandmother
abuelo (m) grandfather
aburrido/a bored, boring
acabar to finish
acampar to camp
acaso perhaps
accidente (m) accident
aceite (m) oil
aceptar to accept
acera pavement
acero (m) steel
acondicionador (de pelo) (m) (hair) conditioner
aconsejar to advise, recommend
actividad (f) activity
acto: en el acto while you wait
acuerdo: de acuerdo agreed, fine, OK
adecuado/a suitable
adelantado: por adelantado in advance
adelante forward, come in!
además besides, as well
adentro indoors
admiten: no se admiten... not allowed...

aduana (f) customs
adulto/a adult
advertir to warn
aéreo/a air
aerodeslizador (m) hovercraft, hydrofoil
aeropuerto (m) airport
afeitar to shave
afilado/a sharp
afuera outside
afueras (f/pl) outskirts
agencia (f) agency
agenda (f) diary
agitado/a rough
agradable pleasant
agradecido/a grateful
agridulce sweet and sour
agrio/a sour
el agua (f) water
agudo/a sharp, acute
aguja (f) needle
agujero (m) hole
ahí there
ahora now
ahumado/a smoked
aire (m) air
aire libre (m) outdoors, open-air
aire acondicionado (m) air conditioning
ajo (m) garlic
ajustado/a tight
al (a+el) to the
albergue (m) hotel, hostel
alcalde (m) mayor
alcázar (m) castle, fortress
alcornoque (m) cork oak
alegre happy
alfiler (m) pin
alfombra (f) carpet
algo anything, something
- » ¿algo más? anything else?

algodón (m) cotton
algodón hidrófilo (m) cotton wool

A

alguien someone
alguno/a any, some
alimentos (m/pl) food
almohada (f) pillow
almuerzo (m) lunch
alojamiento (m) accommodation
alpargata (f) espadrille
alquilar to rent, hire
alrededor (de) around
alrededores (m/pl) surrounding area, outskirts
alto/a height, tall
alumna/o pupil
allá there
allí there
amable kind
amargo/a bitter
amarillo/a yellow
ambiente (m) atmosphere
ambos/as both
amiga (f) female friend
amigo (m) male friend
amueblado/a furnished
anciano/a elderly
ancho/a broad, wide
andando walking, on foot
andén (m) platform
anfiteatro (m) amphitheatre, *(theatre)* circle
anfitrión/a host/hostess
anillo (m) ring
aniversario (m) anniversary
anoche last night
ante (m) suede
antena (f) aerial
antes (de) before
antiadherente non-stick
anticonceptivo (m) contraceptive
antigüedades (f/pl) antiques
anuncio (m) notice, advertisement
año (m) year
apagar to switch/turn off
aparato (m) appliance, machine, device
aparcamiento (m) parking, car park

aparcar to park
apartamento (m) apartment, flat
aparte (de) apart (from), extra
apeadero (m) halt *(railway)*
apellido (m) surname
apenas hardly, scarcely
apetece: ¿le/te apetece…? do you feel like…?
apoyarse to lean
aprender to learn
apretar to push, to press, to tighten
aproveche: ¡que aproveche! enjoy your meal!, bon appétit!
aproximadamente approximately
aquel, aquella that
aquél, aquélla that one
aquellos/as those
aquéllos/as those ones
aquí here
árabe Arab
araña (f) spider
arañazo (m) scratch
árbitro (m) referee
árbol (m) tree
arena (f) sand
armario (m) cupboard
arrancar to tear out, to start *(engine)*, to extract
arreglar to fix, to mend
arriba up, upstairs, above
de arriba upper, top
arroyo (m) stream
el arte (f) art
asado/a roasted
ascensor (m) lift
aseos (m/pl) toilets
así thus, like this/that
asiento (m) seat
áspero/a rough
asunto (m) matter, subject, topic
atacar to attack
atar to tie
atascado/a blocked, jammed
atención (f) beware, take care, attention

atestado/a crowded
atrás behind
» hacia atrás backwards
aumentar increase
aun even
aún still, yet
aunque although
autobús (m) bus
autocar (m) coach
autopista (f) motorway
autostop (m) hitch-hiking
Av, Avda (avenida) (f) avenue
averiado/a broken down, out of order
avión (m) plane
aviso (m) notice, warning
ayer yesterday
ayudar to help
ayuntamiento (m) town hall
azafata (f) air stewardess
azúcar (m) sugar
azúcar moreno (m) brown sugar
azul blue
azul marino navy blue

B

baca (f) roof rack
bahía (f) bay
bailar to dance
bajar to come/go down, to get off
    (bus, etc.), to take down, to turn
    down (volume)
bajo below, under(neath)
bajo/a low, short
balón (m) ball, football
baloncesto (m) basketball
banco (m) bank, bench
bandeja (f) tray
bañera (f) bath(tub)
baño (m) bath
barato/a cheap
barba (f) beard
barca (f) (rowing) boat
barco (m) boat
barquillo (m) ice-cream cone, wafer

barra (f) bar, counter, loaf of bread
barrio (m) district, quarter
basta enough
bastante enough, quite, fairly, quite a lot
bastón (m) walking stick
basura (f) rubbish
batería (f) car battery
baúl (m) trunk
bebé (m) baby
beber to drink
bebida (f) drink
belleza (f) beauty
beso (m) kiss
betún (m) shoe polish
biberón (m) baby's bottle
biblioteca (f) library
bicicleta (f) bicycle
bien well, fine
bigote (m) moustache
billete (m) ticket, banknote
blanco/a white
» en blanco blank
blando/a soft
bloc (m) notepad, writing pad
blusa (f) blouse
boca (f) mouth
bocadillo (m) sandwich
boda (f) wedding
bodega (f) wine cellar, wine shop
bolígrafo (m) ballpoint pen
bolsa (f) bag, stock exchange
bolsillo (m) pocket
bolso (m) handbag
bollo (m) roll
bomba (f) bomb, pump
bomberos (m/pl) fire brigade
bombilla (f) (light)bulb
bombones (m/pl) chocolates
bonito/a pretty, nice, lovely
bordo: a bordo aboard
borracho/a drunk
bosque (m) wood, forest
bota (f) boot
botella (f) bottle

botijo (m) drinking jug with a spout
botón (m) button
botones (m) bellboy
bragas (f/pl) knickers
bravo/a brave, rugged, rough
brazo (m) arm
brillante shiny
brillante (m) diamond
broma (f) joke
bronceado/a (sun-)tanned
buenas *(short for buenos días, buenas tardes, buenas noches)* good morning/afternoon/evening/night
bueno/a, buen good
burro (m) donkey
buscar to look for, to search
butaca (f) armchair, stalls *(theatre)*
buzón (m) postbox

C

C/ (calle) (f) street
caballero (m) gentleman
caballo (m) horse
cabe: no cabe it doesn't fit, it won't go in
cabello (m) hair
cabeza (f) head
cable UBS (m) UBS lead
cabra (f) goat
cacerola (f) saucepan
cada each, every
cadena (f) chain
café (m) coffee
cafetera (f) coffee pot
cafetería (f) café
caja (f) box, cash desk
caja de ahorros (f) savings bank
cajón (m) drawer
calcetines (m) socks
calefacción (f) heating
calentador (m) heater
calidad (f) quality
caliente hot
calor (m) heat

» hace calor it's hot
» tener calor to be hot
calzada (f) roadway, road surface
calzoncillos (m/pl) underpants *(men's)*
callado/a quiet
calle (f) street
¡cállese!, ¡cállate! be quiet!, shut up!
cama (f) bed
cámara (f) camera
camarera (f) waitress
camarero (m) waiter
camarote (m) cabin
cambiar to change
camino (m) track, path, way, route
camisa (f) blouse, shirt
camiseta (f) t-shirt
camisón (m) nightdress
campana (f) bell
campo (m) field, country(side)
canal (m) canal, channel *(TV)*
canción (f) song
cancha (f) court *(tennis, pelota, etc.)*
canguro (m/f) kangaroo, babysitter
cansado/a tired
cantar to sing
cantina (f) buffet, canteen
caña (f) cane, small glass of draught beer
caña de pescar (f) fishing rod
cara (f) face
caramelos (m/pl) sweets
carbón (m) coal
cárcel (f) prison, jail
cardenal (m) bruise
cargo (m) charge, position *(work)*
cariñoso/a affectionate
carne (f) meat
carné/carnet de conducir (m) driving licence
caro/a expensive, dear
carpeta (f) file *(document)*, folder
carrera (f) career, race
carretera (f) road
carril (m) lane *(on road)*
carrito (m) trolley

carta (f) letter, menu

cartas (f/pl) playing cards

cartelera (f) noticeboard, entertainment listings

cartera (f) wallet, purse

carterista (m/f) pickpocket

cartón (m) cardboard, carton

casa (f) house, home

casado/a married

cascada (f) waterfall

cáscara (f) shell, rind, peel

casi almost, nearly

castañuelas (f/pl) castanets

castillo (m) castle

causa: a causa de because of

cena (f) dinner

cenar to have dinner

cenicero (m) ashtray

centro (m) centre, middle

cepillo (m) brush

cerámica (f) pottery

cerdo (m) pig, pork

cerillas (f) matches

cerca (de) close (to), near

cerrado/a closed, blocked

cerradura (f) lock

cerrar to close

césped (m) lawn

cesta (f) basket

chal (m) shawl

chaleco (m) waistcoat

champú (m) shampoo

chándal (m) tracksuit

chaqueta (f) jacket, cardigan

charlar to chat, talk

chica (f) girl

chicle (m) chewing gum

chico (m) boy

chiquito/a, chiquitín/ina very small

chiste (m) joke

chófer (m) driver

choque (m) collision, crash

chupete (m) dummy *(baby's)*

cicatriz (f) scar

ciego/a blind

cielo (m) sky, heaven

cierre (m) fastener, buckle

cifra (f) figure, number

cigarrillo (m) cigarette

cine (m) cinema

cinta (f) ribbon, tape, cassette

cinta métrica (f) tape measure

cintura (f) waist

cinturón (m) belt

circulación (f) traffic, circulation

cita (f) appointment, date

ciudad (f) town, city

claro/a clear, light (coloured), pale

¡claro! of course!

clase (f) class, lesson, type, sort

clavel (m) carnation

clavo (m) nail

cliente (m/f) customer, client

clima (m) climate

climatizado/a air-conditioned

cobrar to charge, to cash

cocina (f) kitchen, cooking

cocinar to cook

coche (m) car

coche de línea (m) coach, long-distance bus

cochecito (de niño) (m) pram

código (m) code

coger to take, catch, get

cola (f) tail, queue, glue

colchón (m) mattress

colgar to hang up, to hang

colina (f) hill

color (m) colour

combinación (f) combination, connection, plan

comedor (m) dining-room

comer to eat

comestibles (m) food, groceries

comida (f) food, meal, lunch

comisaría (f) police station

como like, as

¿cómo? pardon?

¿cómo...? how...?
cómodo/a comfortable
compañía (f) company
completamente completely
completo/a complete, full (up)
comprar to buy
compras (f/pl) shopping
compresas (f/pl) sanitary towels
comprobar to check
compromiso (m) obligation,
   appointment, engagement
común common
con with
concurso (m) competition, contest
conducir to drive
conductor (m) driver
congelado/a (deep) frozen
congreso (m) conference, congress
conjunto (m) group
conmigo with me
conocer to know, be acquainted with
» conozco I know
conseguir to obtain, get
conservar to keep
conservas (f) tinned food
constipado/a: estar constipado/a to
   have a cold
contador (m) meter
contaminación (f) pollution
contenido (m) contents
contento/a pleased
contestar to answer
contigo with you
contra against
conviene: no me conviene it doesn't suit
   me, it's not convenient
copa (f) cup, glass, drink
corazón (m) heart
corbata (f) tie
cordero (m) lamb
corona (f) crown
corcho (m) cork
Correos post office
correr to run

correspondencia (f) connection,
   correspondence
corriente (f) (electrical) power, current
cortar to cut, cut off
las Cortes (f/pl) Spanish Parliament
cortina (f) curtain
corto/a short
cosa (f) thing
cosecha (f) harvest, vintage
costa (f) coast
costar to cost
coto (m) (hunting) reserve
creer to think, believe
» creo que sí/no I think so/
   I don't think so
crema (f) cream, lotion
cremallera (f) zip
crimen (m) crime
cruce (m) crossroads, junction
crucero (m) cruise
crudo/a raw
cruz (f) cross
cruzar to cross
cuaderno (m) exercise book
cuadro (m) picture, painting, square, check
¿cuál?, ¿cuáles? which?
cualquier(a) any, whichever
¿cuándo? when?
¿cuánto/a? how much?
¿cuántos/as? how many?
» ¿cuántos años tiene? how old is
   he/she?, how old are you? (formal)
» ¿cuánto tiempo? how long? (time)
cuarto (m) quarter, room
cubierta (f) cover, deck
cubierto/a covered, overcast (weather)
cubiertos (m) cutlery
cubo (m) bucket, bin
cubrir to cover
cuchara (f) spoon
cuchillo (m) knife
cuello (m) neck, collar
cuenta (f) bill, account
cuento (m) story, tale

cuerda (f) rope, string
cuero (m) leather
cuerpo (m) body
cuesta, cuestan it costs, they cost
cueva (f) cave
cuidado: tener cuidado to take care
cuidar to look after
culpa (f) fault
cumpleaños (m) birthday
cuñada (f) sister-in-law
cuñado (m) brother-in-law
cura (m) priest
cuyo/a whose

D

D (don) Mr *(courtesy title for man)*
Dña (doña) Mrs *(courtesy title for woman)*
daño (m) damage
dar to give
de of, from, about
debajo (de) under, underneath
débil weak
decidir to decide
décimo/a tenth
decir to say, to tell
» es decir that's to say, in other words
dedo (m) finger
dedo del pie (m) toe
degustación (f) tasting, sampling
dejar to leave
del (de+el) of the
delante (de) in front (of)
delantero/a front
delgado/a slim
demás rest
demasiado/a too (much)
demora (f) delay
dentífrico (m) toothpaste
dentro (de) in, inside
denunciar to report
deporte (m) sport
derecha/o right
derechos (de aduana) (m/pl) (customs)
    duty

desagradable unpleasant
desayuno (m) breakfast
descalzo/a barefoot
descanso (m) rest, interval, half-time
desconocido/a unknown, strange
describir to describe
descubrir to discover
descuento (m) discount
desear to want, to wish
desde from
desde luego of course
desgracia (f) misfortune, accident
desgraciadamente unfortunately
desnudo/a naked, nude
despacio slowly
despacho (m) office
después after(wards), later
después de after
destino (m) destination
destornillador (m) screwdriver
desventaja (f) disadvantage
detrás (de) behind
devolver to give back, return
día (m) day
día festivo (m) *(public)* holiday
día laboral (m) weekday
diapositiva (f) slide *(photo)*
diario/a daily
dibujo (m) drawing
dibujos animados (m) cartoon film
diente (m) tooth
difícil difficult
¿diga?, ¿dígame? hello *(on phone)*,
    can I help you? *(in shops, etc.)*
digamos let's say
digital digital
dinero (m) money
dirección (f) direction, address
disco (m) disc, record
disco duro (m) hard drive
discrecional optional
discusión (f) discussion, argument
diseño (m) drawing, design
distinto/a different

divertido/a funny, amusing

doblar to turn

doble double

dodotis (m/pl) disposable nappies

dolor pain, ache

¿dónde? where?

dormir to sleep

dormitorio (m) bedroom

dos two

los/las dos both

doy I give

ducha (f) shower

duele (it) hurts

dueño/a owner

dulce sweet

durante during

duro/a hard

E

echar to throw (away), to put in

edad (f) age

edificio (m) building

EEUU=Estados Unidos (m) United States

efectivamente really, in fact, exactly

eficaz effective

ejemplo (m) example

el the

él he, him

ella she, her

ellas they, them

ello it

ellos they, them

email (m) email

embajada (f) embassy

embalse (m) reservoir

embarazada pregnant

embarcadero (m) pier, jetty

embarque (m) boarding

embutidos (m/pl) sausages, cold meats

emisora (f) radio station

emocionante exciting

empezar to begin

emplear to use, employ

empresa (f) firm, business

empujar to push

en in, on

encantado/a delighted

encendedor (m) (cigarette) lighter

encender to light, switch/turn on

encima (de) on top (of)

encontrar to find, to meet

enchufe (m) plug, socket

energía (f) energy, power

enfadado/a angry, annoyed

enfermo/a ill

enfrente (de) opposite

¡enhorabuena! congratulations!

enorme enormous

enseñanza (f) teaching, education

enseñar to teach, to show

entender to understand

entero/a whole

entiendo I understand

entonces then

la entrada entrance, admission, ticket

entrar (en) to enter, go in

entre among, between

entrega (f) delivery

entresuelo (m) circle (theatre)

envase (m) container

enviar to send

equipaje (m) luggage, baggage

equipo (m) team, equipment

equivocado/a mistaken, wrong

es he/she/it is, you are (formal)

escalera (f) stairs, staircase

escaparate (m) shop window

escarpado/a steep

escoba (f) broom

esconder to hide

escribir to write

escuchar to listen (to)

escuela (f) school

ese/a that

ése/a that one

eso that (one)

esos/as those

ésos/as those ones

esmalte (m) varnish, enamel
espacio (m) space
espantoso/a awful, dreadful
España Spain
español/ola Spanish
esparadrapo (m) plaster
especia (f) spice
especial special, peculiar
especie (f) type, kind, species
espectáculo (m) show, spectacle
espejo (m) mirror
esperar to wait/hope (for), to expect
esposa (f) wife
esposo (m) husband
espuma (f) foam
esquí (m) ski, skiing
esquiar to ski
esquina (f) corner
está he/she/it is, you are *(formal)*
estación (f) station, season
estacionamiento (m) parking
estadio (m) stadium
estado (m) state
estancia (f) stay
estanco (m) tobacconist's
estar to be
este (m) east
este/a this
éste/a this one
esto this (one)
estómago (m) stomach
estos/as these
éstos/as these ones
estoy I am
estrecho/a narrow, tight
estrella (f) star
estreno (m) première, first performance
estropeado/a broken down, out of order
estufa (f) stove
éxito (m) success
explicar to explain
exposición (f) exhibition
extranjero (m) abroad
extranjero/a foreign

extraño/a strange, odd
euro (m) euro

F

fábrica (f) factory
fácil easy
facturación (f) check-in
falda (f) skirt
falso/a false, fake
falta (f) lack
» hace falta... ...is needed
familia (f) family
farol (m) street lamp
FC (ferrocarril) (m) railway
fecha (f) date
feliz happy
feo/a ugly
feria (f) fair
fiambres (m/pl) cold meats
fiebre (f) fever, (high) temperature
fiesta (f) festival, holiday
fila (f) row, tier
filial (f) branch
fin (m) end
fin de semana (m) weekend
finca (f) (country) estate
firmar to sign
flaco/a thin
flojo/a slack, loose, flabby
flor (f) flower
folleto (m) leaflet, brochure
fontanero (m) plumber
forma (f) form, shape
» de todas formas anyway
fósforos (m) matches
frase (f) phrase, sentence
fregar los platos to do the washing-up
frente a facing, faced with
fresco/a fresh, cool
frigorífico (m) refrigerator
frío/a cold
» hace frío it's cold *(weather)*
» tener frío to be cold
frito/a fried

frontera (f) border, frontier
fuego (m) fire, light *(for cigarette)*
fuente (f) fountain
fuera (de) outside
fuerte strong, loud
fuerza (f) strength, power
fumar to smoke
funcionar to work, function
funda (de la almohada) (f) (pillow)case
furgoneta (f) van

G

gafas (f/pl) glasses, spectacles
galleta (f) biscuit
ganar to earn, to win
garganta (f) throat
gaseosa (f) lemonade
gasolina (f) petrol
gastar to spend
gato (m) cat
GC (Guardia Civil) (f) Civil Guard
gente (f) people
gerente (m) manager
gitano/a gypsy
gobierno (m) government
golpe (m) knock, blow
goma (f) rubber
gordo/a fat
gota (f) drop
grabar to record
gracias thank you
gracioso/a funny
grado (m) degree *(temperature)*
gran, grande big, large, great
Gran Bretaña Great Britain
grandes almacenes (m) department
  store
granja (f) farm
gratis free
grave serious
grifo (m) tap
gripe (f) flu
gris grey, dull
grito (m) shout, cry

grosero/a rude
grúa (f) tow truck
grueso/a thick
guante (m) glove
guapo/a good-looking
guardar to keep
guardarropa (m) cloakroom
guardia: de guardia on duty
guerra (f) war
guía (m/f) guide, guidebook
gusta: me gusta/gustan I like
 » le gusta/gustan he/she/it likes,
    you like *(formal)*
gusto: mucho gusto it's a pleasure
    (to meet you)

H

habitación (f) room
hablar to speak, to talk
hace he/she/it does/make, you do/
    make *(formal)*
hace ... (años) ...(years) ago
hacer to do, to make
hacia towards
hago I do/make
hamaca (f) deckchair
hambre (f) hunger
 » tener hambre to be hungry
hasta until, as far as, even, including
hasta luego/pronto see you soon,
    so long
hay... there is/are...
¿hay... ? Is/are there... ?
 » ¿qué hay? how are things?
 » hay que you have to, you must,
    it is necessary to
hecho (m) fact
hecho/a done, made, cooked
helado (m) ice-cream
herido/a injured, wounded
hermana (f) sister
hermano (m) brother
hermoso/a beautiful
hervido/a boiled

hielo (m) ice
hierba (f) grass, herb
hierro (m) iron
hija (f) daughter
hijo (m) son
hilo (m) thread
hogar (m) home, house, household
hola hello, hi
hombre (m) man
hora (f) hour
horario (m) timetable
horas puntas (f/pl) rush hours
horno (m) oven
hoy today
huele it smells
huelga (f) strike
huésped (m) guest
hueso (m) bone
huevo (m) egg
húmedo/a damp
humo (m) smoke

I

ida (solamente) single, one-way *(ticket)*
ida y vuelta return
idioma (m) language
iglesia (f) church
igual equal, the same
» me da igual I don't mind
impermeable waterproof
impermeable (m) raincoat
importa: no importa it doesn't matter
importe (m) amount
imprescindible essential
impresionante impressive
imprevisto/a unexpected
incendio (m) fire
incluido/a included
incluso/a included, including
incómodo/a uncomfortable
inconveniente (m) problem
infierno (m) hell
informe (m) report
inglés, inglesa English

inquilino/a tenant
insolación (f) sunstroke
insólito/a unusual
instantáneo/a instant
interés (m) interest *(money)*
interruptor (m) switch
introducir to introduce, to insert
inútil useless
invierno (m) winter
ir to go
isla (f) island
IVA (m) VAT
izquierda (f) left
izquierdo/a left

J

jabón (m) soap
jamás never
jamón (m) ham
jarabe (m) syrup
jardín (m) garden
jarra (f) jug
jefe (m/f) boss, head, chief
jerez (m) sherry
jornada (f) day
joven young
joven (m/f) young person
jubilado/a retired
judía (f) bean
juego (m) game, gambling, set, collection
jugar to play
juguete (m) toy
junto/a together
¡justo! that's right!
justo/a fair, just, correct, exact
juventud (f) youth

L

la the, her, it
lado (m) side
» al lado de beside, next to
lago (m) lake
lámpara (f) lamp
lana (f) wool

lanzar to throw
lápiz (m) pencil
largo/a long
las the, them
lástima: ¡qué lástima! what a pity!
lata (f) tin, can
lavabo (m) wash-basin, toilet
lavandería (f) launderette
lavar to wash
le him, (to) him/her/it, (to)
    you *(formal)*
lectura (f) reading
leche (f) milk
leer to read
lejos far (away)
lengua (f) tongue, language
lento/a slow
les (to) them, (to) you *(formal)*
levantar to lift, raise
ley (f) law
libra (esterlina) (f) pound (sterling)
libre free, unoccupied, vacant, for hire
librería (f) bookshop
libro (m) book
ligero/a light
lima (f) file, lime
limpiar to clean
limpiar en seco to dry-clean
limpio/a clean
línea (f) line
liso/a smooth
listo/a ready, clever
litera (f) berth, couchette
litoral (m) coast
llamada (f) call
llamar to call
» ¿cómo se llama (usted)? what is
    your name?
llave (f) key
llave inglesa (f) spanner
llegada (f) arrival
llegar (a) to arrive (at), reach
lleno/a full (up)
llevar to carry, to take (away), to wear

llorar to cry
lloviendo: está lloviendo it's raining
lluvia (f) rain
lo it, him
localidad (f) place, seat, ticket, town
loción (f) lotion
loco/a crazy, mad
Londres London
los the, them
lotería (f) lottery
luego then
lugar (m) place
lujo: de lujo de luxe, luxury
luna (f) moon
luz (f) light, electricity

M

madera (f) wood
madre (f) mother
maduro/a mature, ripe
maestro/a (primary school) teacher
mal badly
maleta (f) suitcase
malo/a, mal bad
mancha (f) stain
mandar to send
manera (f) way, manner
manga (f) sleeve
manifestación (f) protest
mano (f) hand
manta (f) blanket
manzanilla (f) camomile tea, dry sherry
mañana tomorrow
mañana (f) morning
maquillaje (m) make-up
máquina (f) machine
mar (m) sea
marca (f) make, brand
marchar to go
» me marcho I'm going/leaving
marido (m) husband
mariscos (m/pl) shellfish
marrón brown
martillo (m) hammer

más more, plus
matar to kill
matrícula (f) registration number
matrimonio (m) marriage
mayor elder, bigger, main
mayor parte (f) most
mayoría (f) majority
me (to) me
mechero (m) (cigarette) lighter
medianoche (f) midnight
mediante using, by means of
medias (f/pl) stockings, tights
médico (m) doctor
medida (m) measurement, size
medio/a half
medio ambiente (m) environment
mediodía (m) midday
mejor better, best
menor smaller, smallest, least
menos less, minus
» por lo menos at least
mensaje de texto (m) text message
menudo: a menudo often
mercado (m) market
merienda (f) snack, picnic, tea
mermelada (f) jam
mes (m) month
mesa (f) table
meter to put
mezcla (f) mixture
mezquita (f) mosque
mi my
mí me
microondas (m) microwave (oven)
miedo: tener miedo to be afraid
miembro (m/f) member
mientras while
mientras tanto meanwhile
minusválido/a disabled
mío/a mine
mirar to look (at), to watch
mis my *(pl)*
misa (f) mass
mismo/a same, self

mitad (f) half
mixto/a mixed
mochila (f) rucksack
moda (f) fashion
módem (m) modem
modo (m) way, manner
mojado/a wet
molestar to bother, annoy
molino (m) mill
moneda (f) currency, coin
monedero (m) purse
montaña (f) mountain
montar to ride
monte (m) mountain
montón: un montón (de), montones
    a lot (of), lots
morado/a purple
moreno/a dark *(hair/skin)*
mosca (f) fly
mostrar to show
moto(cicleta) (f) motorbike
mover to move
móvil (m) mobile phone
muchacha (f) girl
muchacho (m) boy
mucho very (much), a lot
mucho/a a lot (of)
muchos/as many, lots (of)
muebles (m) furniture
muelle (m) quay, pier
muerto/a dead
mujer (f) woman, wife
multa (f) fine
mundo (m) world
muñeca (f) wrist, doll
muro (m) wall
musulmán/a Muslim
muy very

N

nada nothing
» de nada not at all, don't mention it
nadar to swim
nadie no-one, nobody

naipes (m/pl) playing cards

naranja (f) orange; orange *(colour)*

nariz (f) nose

natación (f) swimming

Navidad (f) Christmas

necesitar to need

negocios (m/pl) business

negro/a black

nevera (f) refrigerator

ni nor

ni... ni neither... nor

ni siquiera not even

niebla (f) fog

nieta (f) granddaughter

nieto (m) grandson

nieve (f) snow

ninguno/a, ningún no, not any

» en ninguna parte nowhere

niña (f) girl

niño (m) boy

no no, not

noche (f) night

nombre (m) name

norte (m) north

nos us

nosotros/as we, us

noticias (f/pl) news

novia (f) girlfriend, fiancée

novio (m) boyfriend, fiancé

nublado/a cloudy

nuera (f) daughter-in-law

nuestro/a our, ours

nuevo: de nuevo again

nuevo/a new

número (m) number, size *(shoe)*

nunca never

O

o... o... either ... or...

obra (f) work, play *(theatre)*

ocupado/a occupied, engaged

oeste (m) west

oferta (f) offer

oficina (f) office

oído (m) hearing, ear

¡oiga!, ¡oye! listen!, hello!

ojo (m) eye

ola (f) wave

olor (m) smell

onda (f) wave *(radio, hair)*

ordenado/a tidy

ordenador (m) computer

oreja (f) ear

oro (m) gold

os you, to you

otoño (m) autumn

otra vez again

otro/a another, other

oveja (f) sheep

oxiado/a rusty

¡oye! listen! hello!

P

padre (m) father

padres (m/pl) parents

pagar to pay (for)

página (f) page

país (m) country

paisaje (m) countryside, scenery

pájaro (m) bird

palabra (f) word

pálido/a pale, light *(colour)*

palo (m) stick, pole, (golf) club

pan (m) bread

pantalón (m)/pantalones (m/pl) trousers

pantalla (f) screen

pañales (m/pl) nappies

paño (m) cloth

pañuelo (m) handkerchief

papel (m) paper

para for, in order to

parada (f) stop, (taxi) rank

paraguas (m) umbrella

parar to stop

parecer to seem

pared (f) wall

pareja (f) couple

pariente/a relation, relative
paro (m) unemployment
parque (m) park
parte (f) part
partido (m) *(political)* party, match
pasado/a past, last
pasajero (m) passenger
pasar to pass, to spend *(time)*, to happen
pasatiempo (m) pastime, hobby
Pascua (f) Easter
paseo (m) walk, ride
pasillo (m) corridor, aisle
paso a nivel (m) level crossing
paso de peatones (m) pedestrian crossing
pasta de dientes (f) toothpaste
pastel (m) cake, pastry
patines (m/pl) skates
paz (f) peace
peaje (m) toll
peatón (m) pedestrian
pedazo (m) piece
pedir to ask (for)
peine (m) comb
película (f) film
peligro (m) danger
pelo (m) hair
pelota (f) ball, Basque national ball-game
peluquería (f) hairdresser's, barber's
pena (f) shame, pity
 » ¡qué pena! what a pity!
pensar to think
pensión (f) pension, boarding house
peor worse, worst
pequeño/a small, little
perder to lose, to miss
perdone, perdón pardon me/excuse me
perezoso/a lazy
periódico (m) newspaper
periodista (m/f) journalist
permiso (m) licence, perrnit
permitido/a allowed
pero but
perro (m) dog
persona (f) person

pesado/a heavy, boring, tedious
pescado (m) fish
peso (m) weight
picante hot, spicy
picar to sting, bite
pie (m) foot
piedra (f) stone
piel (f) skin, fur, leather
pierna (f) leg
pila (f) battery
píldora (f) pill
pimienta (f) pepper
pintar to paint
pintura (f) paint, painting
piscina (f) swimming pool
piso (m) floor, storey, flat
pista (f) track, course, (ski-)run
plancha (f) iron, sailboard
planta (f) plant, floor, storey
plata (f) silver
platillo (m) saucer
plato (m) dish, course
playa (f) beach
plaza (f) square
plaza de toros (f) bullring
plomo (m) lead
pobre poor
poco/a little, not much
pocos/as few, not many
poder to be able
podrido/a rotten
policía (f) police
política (f) politics
pollo (m) chicken
poner to put, to place, to put down
por by, for, per, through, via
por ejemplo (p. ej.) for example (e.g.)
por favor please
¿por qué? why?
porque because
postal (f) postcard
postre (m) dessert
precio (m) price
precioso/a lovely

preciso/a precise, exact, necessary
preferir to prefer
preguntar to ask
premio (m) prize
preocupado/a worried
preparar to prepare, get ready
presentar to introduce
préstamo (m) loan
primavera (f) spring
primero/a, primer first
primo/a cousin
principiante (m/f) beginner
principio (m) beginning
prisa: tener prisa to be in a hurry
privado/a private
problema (m) problem
procedencia (f) point of departure
profesor/a teacher, lecturer, professor
profundo/a deep
prohibido/a prohibited, forbidden
pronto soon
propietario/a owner, landlady, landlord
propina (f) tip
próximo/a next
público/a public
pueblo (m) people, village
puede he/she/it can, you can (formal)
puedo I can
puente (m) bridge
puerta (f) door, gate
puerto (m) port, harbour, docks
pulgar (m) thumb
pulsar to press, push
pulsera (f) bracelet
puñado (m) handful, fistful
    puro (m) cigar

Q

que that, which, than
¿qué? what?, which?
¿qué tal? how are things?, how are you?
quemar to burn
querer to want, to love
queso (m) cheese

¿quién?, ¿quiénes? who?
quiere decir it means
quiero I want, I love
quisiera I would like, you would like,
    he/she would like
quitar to remove, take away
quizá/quizás perhaps, maybe

R

raro/a rare, odd
razón (f) reason
» tiene(s) razón you are right
real royal
realidad: en realidad in fact
rebaja (f) reduction, sale
recado (m) message
receta (f) recipe, prescription
recibo (m) receipt
reclamación (f) complaint
recogida (f) collection
recto, todo recto straight on
recuerdo (m) memory, souvenir
red (f) net, network
redondo/a round
reembolso (m) refund
refresco (m) cold drink
regalo (m) gift, present
régimen (m) diet
región (f) region, area
regla (f) ruler, period
reina (f) queen
reloj (m) clock, watch
rellenar to fill (in)
remedio (m) remedy, cure
remolcar to tow
RENFE (f) Spanish railway
    network
reparar to repair
repente: de repente suddenly
repetir to repeat
reportaje (m) report
representación (f) performance
repuesto (m) spare part, replacement
resbaladizo/a slippery

reserva (f) reservation, booking
reservar to reserve, book
resfriado (m) cold *(illness)*
respuesta (f) answer, reply
resultado (m) result
retraso (m) delay
retrete (m) toilet
revelar to show, to develop *(film)*
revés: al revés the wrong way round, upside down, inside out
revisar to check
revista (f) magazine
rey (m) king
rico/a rich, delicious
rincón (m) córner
río (m) river
risa (f) laugh
rizado/a curly
robar to rob, to steal
rodeado/a (de) surrounded *(by)*
rojo/a red
rollo (m) (roll of) film
romper to break
ropa (f) clothes, clothing
ropa interior (f) underwear
rosa pink
rosa (f) rose
roto/a broken
rubio/a fair, blond(e)
rueda (f) wheel
ruido (m) noise
ruina (f) ruin

S

S (San) Saint
sábana (f) sheet
saber to know (how to)
sabor (m) taste, flavour
sacacorchos (m) corkscrew
sacar to get/take out, to remove
sacerdote (m) priest
sal (f) salt
sala (f) room, lounge, (concert) hall
salado/a salty, savoury

salgo I go out/am going out
salida (f) exit, way out, departure
salir to come/go out, to leave, depart
salón (m) lounge, living-room
saltar to jump
salud (f) health
¡salud! cheers!
salvaje wild
salvar to rescue, save
sangre (f) blood
sano/a healthy
san, santo, santa saint
sartén (f) frying pan
se him/her/itself, yourself, themselves
sé, no sé I know, I don't know
secar to dry
seco/a dry
sed (f) thirst
» tener sed to be thirsty
seda (f) silk
seguida: en seguida immediately
seguido/a continuous
según according to, depending on
segundo/a second
seguro (m) insurance
seguro/a sure, certain, safe
sello (m) stamp
semáforo (m) traffic lights
semana (f) week
sencillo/a simple
sendero (m) path
sensato/a sensible
sentado/a sitting (down)
sentido (m) sense, feeling
sentir to feel
señal (f) sign, signal
señas (f) address
señor (m) gentleman, Mr
señora (f) lady, Mrs
señorita (f) young lady, Miss
ser to be
serio/a serious
seropositivo/a HIV positive
servicio (m) service, service charge

servicios (m/pl) toilets
servilleta (f) napkin, serviette
servir to serve
sesión (f) session, *(cinema)* screening
si if, whether
sí yes
SIDA (m) AIDS
siempre always
siento: lo siento I'm sorry
sierra (f) saw, mountain range
siglo (m) century
significado (m) meaning
siguiente following, next
silencioso/a silent
silla (f) chair
silla de ruedas (f) wheelchair
sillita de paseo (f) push-chair
simpático/a nice, charming, pleasant
sin without
sin embargo however
sino but (rather)
sinvergüenza (m/f) rascal, scoundrel
sitio (m) place
sobre on, upon, about
sobre (m) envelope
sobre todo above all, especially
sobrina (f) niece
sobrino (m) nephew
software (m) software
sol (m) sun, sunshine
solamente only
solicitar to apply for
sólo only
solo/a alone, lonely
soltero/a single, unmarried
sombra (f) shade, shadow
sonrisa (f) smile
sopa (f) soup
sordo/a deaf
sorpresa (f) surprise
sostén (m) bra
sótano (m) basement
soy I am
Sr (señor) (m) Mr

Sra (señora) (f) Mrs
Sres (señores) (m) Mr and Mrs
Srta (señorita) (f) Miss
Sta (Santa) (f) Saint
Sto (Santo) (m) Saint
su, sus his/her/its, their, your
suave smooth, mild, gentle
subir to come/go up, to lift up, take up
subterráneo/a underground
sucio/a dirty
sucursal (f) branch *(of bank, etc.)*
suegra (f) mother-in-law
suegro (m) father-in-law
sueldo (m) wage
suelo (m) floor, ground
suelto (m) (small) change
sueño (m) sleep, dream
tener sueño to be sleepy
suerte (f) luck
tener suerte to be lucky
» ¡buena suerte! good luck!
supositorio (m) suppository
supuesto: por supuesto of course
sur (m) south
susto (m) fright, scare
suyo/a his/her/its, theirs, yours

T

tal such
talla (f) size
taller (m) workshop, garage
tamaño (m) size
también also, as well, too
tampoco neither
tan so
tanto/a so much
tantos/as so many
tapa (f) lid, snack, appetiser
tapón (m) plug
taquilla (f) booking office, box office
tardar to take (time)
tarde late
tarde (f) afternoon, evening
tarjeta (f) card

tarro (m) pot, jar
tarta (f) cake, gâteau, tart, pie
taza (f) cup
teatro (m) theatre
techo (m) ceiling
tejado (m) roof
tejido (m) fabric, textile, weave
tela (f) fabric, material
teleférico (m) cable car
temporada (f) season
temprano early
tenedor (m) fork
tener to have
» tengo I have
» tengo que I must, I have to
tercero/a, tercer third
terraza (f) terrace
testigo (m/f) witness
tía (f) aunt
tiempo (m) time, weather
tienda (f) shop, tent
tiene he/she/it has, you have (formal)
tiene que he/she/it must, has to, you
    must, you have to (formal)
tierra (f) earth, land, ground
tijeras (f/pl) scissors
timbre (m) bell
tinto/a red (wine)
tío (m) uncle, bloke, guy (slang)
tipo (m) type, sort, kind, chap
tirar to throw, to throw away, to pull
tiritas (f/pl) plasters
toalla (f) towel
tocador dressing table, powder room
tocar to touch, to play (instrument)
todavía yet, still
todo everything
todo/a, todos/as all, every
todo el mundo everyone
tomar to take, to have (to drink)
tonelada (f) ton
torcido/a twisted, sprained
tormenta (f) (thunder)storm
tornillo (m) screw

toro (m) bull
torre (f) tower
tos (f) cough
trabajar to work
trabajo (m) work, job
traducir to translate
traje (m) dress, suit, outfit
traje de baño (m) swimsuit
trampolín (m) diving board
tranquilo/a calm, quiet
transbordo transfer
trapo (m) cloth, rag
tras after, behind
trasero/a rear, back
tratar to treat, to deal with
» se trata de... it's to do with...
través: a través de through, across
tren (m) train
tripulación (f) crew
triste sad, unhappy
trozo (m) piece, bit
tu, tus your
tú you
tumbona (f) deckchair
turno (m) turn, shift
tuyo/a yours

U

Ud, Uds (usted, ustedes) you
UE (Unión Europea) EU, European Union
ulema (m) mullah
últimamente lately
último/a last, latest
un a/an, one
una a/an, one
único/a unique, only
universidad (f) university
uno one
unos/as some
uña (f) nail
urbanización (f) urban development
uso (m) use, usage, custom
usted, ustedes you (formal)
útil useful
utilizar to use

V

va he/she/it goes/is going, you go/are going *(formal)*
vaca (f) cow
vacaciones (f/pl) holiday(s)
vacío/a empty
vagón (m) carriage *(train)*
vajilla (f) crockery, dishes
vale fine, OK
» vale la pena it's worth it
valiente brave
valle (m) valley
vapor (m) steam
vaqueros (m/pl) jeans
varios/as several, some
vaso (m) glass
Vd, Vds (usted, ustedes) you *(formal)*
veces (f) *(pl of vez)* times
» a veces sometimes
» muchas veces many times
vecino/a neighbour
vela (f) candle, sail, sailing
velocidad (f) speed
vencer to defeat, beat
vender to sell
veneno (m) poison
venir to come
venta (f) sale, country inn
ventaja (f) advantage
ventana (f) window
ver to see
verano (m) summer
veras: ¿de veras? really?
verbena (f) verbena, local open-air festival
verdad (f) truth
» ¿verdad? right?, true?, isn't that so?
verde green
verdura (f) green vegetables, greenery
verificar to check
vestido (m) dress
vez (f) time
» a la vez at the same time
» en vez de instead of
» otra vez again
viajar to travel
viaje (m) journey, trip
vida (f) life
vidrio (m) glass
viejo/a old
viento (m) wind
VIH (m) HIV
vino (m) wine
viña (f) vineyard
viraje (m) bend, curve
visita (f) visit
visitar to visit
vista (f) (eye)sight, look, view
viuda (f) widow
viudo (m) widower
¡viva…! long live…!, up with…!
vivienda (f) housing
vivir to live
vivo/a live, alive, vivid, bright
volumen (m) volume
volver to return
vosotros/as you
voy I go/am going
voz (f) voice
vuelo (m) flight
vuelta (f) turn, return
vuestro/a your, yours

Y

y and
ya already, now
» ¡ya! of course!
yerno (m) son-in-law
yo I

Z

zapatillas (f/pl) trainers, sports shoes
zapato (m) shoe
zarzuela (f) Spanish light opera
zumo (m) juice

index

index

223

Now you're talking!

If you're keen to progress to a higher level, BBC Active offers a wide range of innovative products, from short courses and grammars to build up your vocabulary and confidence to more in-depth courses for beginners or intermediates. Designed by language-teaching experts, our courses make the best use of today's technology, with book and audio, audio-only and multi-media products on offer.

Independent, interactive study course
2 x PC CD-ROM; 144pp course book, 60-min audio CD; online activities and resources

Get Into Spanish is an interactive language course for people on the go. Available as a complete course on CD-ROM, supported by a book, audio CD and web site, its flexible approach puts you firmly in control of how, when and where you learn. Based around a virtual Spanish town complete with hotel, restaurant, shops and more, it allows you to take part in on-screen conversations and improve your language skills in an environment second only to the real thing.
Also available: Get Into French.

Short independent study course
128pp course book;
2 x 60-min CDs;
free online activities;
6-part television series

Short audio course
2 x 70-min CDs

BBC ACTIVE